Past & Present Ireland
a new perspective

Ireland is an enchanting land where the legacies of the Celtic civilisation, of the holy saints and mythical heroes have mingled over the centuries to weave an atmosphere redolent of the mysticism that pervades the country. From the dignity of its splendid Georgian architecture to the bleakness of the bone coloured Burren, from the seductive vistas of lush emerald green to the unforgiving wilds of Connemara, Ireland is suffused with ineffable charm and a beguiling beauty.

During the course of Ireland's tragic and turbulent past the distinctions between legend and history have, on occasion, become as blurred as the soft outlines of the mist-shrouded Irish landscapes: Past & Present Ireland casts a new light on the enigmas of Ireland's ancient culture and heritage and on the consequences of the Irishman's lyrical pattern for his country that once led even a simple farmer to 'make his field a bride'.

Past & Present Ireland

by Sarah Newitt

Cover Illustration Liz Wright

Published in the United Kingdom
by Ptarmigan Publishing Ltd

Growers Court
New Road
Bromham, Chippenham
Wiltshire SN15 2JA

Telephone: 01380 -859983
Facsimile: 01380 -859682

ISBN 0 9526380 2 9

British Library Cataloguing in Publication Data. A catalogue record for this book is available from the British Library.

Acknowledgments
Gary McGovern, Mark Fiennes, John Kehely at Kee Wi Photo, Bord Fáilte/Irish Tourist Board, Northern Irish Tourist Board, The Bridgeman Art Library

Contents

Ireland - a brief history

Some 8,000 years ago the densely and more or less impenetrably forested country of Ireland was colonised around the coast by immigrants from Britain. These hunter gatherers arrived over land bridges, which were submerged a thousand years later at the end of the last ice age to confer on Ireland the island status which has shaped so much of its history and character. From 3500 BC, Neolithic peoples from the European seaboard introduced farming and built the strange and wonderful passage graves which abound in the Boyne Valley. Their comparatively advanced culture was subsequently overshadowed by the Bronze Age Beaker People, whose adroit goldworking skills were famed throughout Europe and whose sophisticated bronze artefacts revolutionised military and domestic life.

From about 400 BC the Celts, known as the Galli by the Romans, settled Ireland, having been chased from central Europe by the expanding Roman Empire. However, rather than obliterating the customs and mythology of their predecessors, the Celts assimilated the existing mores of their adopted country in the first of several cultural fusions which eventually generated the unique spirit of Ireland as it is today. Despite the undisputed warrior instincts of these invaders, the indigenous Irish must have accepted their subjugation with some equanimity, there being little evidence of violent struggle in the process.

Celtic society was based on small kingdoms grouped into the Five Fifths of Ulster, Meath, Leinster, Munster and Connaught, which were theoretically, although rarely in reality, ruled by a High King from Tara in County Meath. The intense sanctity of Tara bore little relation to the lack of political power vested in the position of High King, but none the less the Celts, or Gaels, were united by a common law, a common language and a compelling common tradition of poetry and music which had already formed the basis of a coherent Irish cultural identity and which remained unadulterated by the classical influence of the Roman empire. As one author wrote, the Roman lack of interest in Ireland was one of the greatest non-events in Irish history.

In the fifth century, Christianity came to Ireland, largely as a result of the British St Patrick who, despite a somewhat inauspicious introduction to the Irish - he was kidnapped at the age of 16 by Irish pirates and forced to work as a slave tending sheep - charitably returned several years later to convert his abductors. As the Romans withdrew from England and Europe plunged into the Dark Ages, Ireland conversely entered a Golden Age, becoming an influential and inspirational centre of Christianity, learning and the arts. Great monasteries were built, Irish missionaries such as St Columba became leading lights in the dissemination of the Christian word and Gaelic culture flourished in another triumph of fusion, this time

Wedge tomb
Lough Gur

with Christianity, its apotheosis embodied in the exquisite Book of Kells. Ireland became known as the land of "Saints and Scholars" and notwithstanding frequent territorial wranglings between the Celtic tribes, life was relatively stable.

All this changed abruptly at the end of the eighth century when the Viking vogue for raid and incursion propelled Ireland into chaos. Danes penetrated the heart of the country by navigating the waterways, plundering the monasteries and shattering what peace there was with a ferocity previously unencountered in Ireland. Undeterred by any form of coordinated resistance, the Vikings dominated the scene for several hundred years and founded the first major Irish towns, many of them at river mouths, such as Dublin, a tenth century Viking kingdom, Wexford and Cork. Their stranglehold was finally broken in 1014 by Brian Boru, the last High King to hold any degree of jurisdiction over Ireland, who unequivocally defeated the Vikings at the Battle of Clontarf, whilst simultaneously disposing of some of his own more troublesome Irish enemies. Boru was murdered shortly after the battle and the ensuing tussle for the position of High King reduced Ireland to a state of turmoil and unrest, during which time the remaining Vikings abandoned their hostile stance and gradually became fully integrated into Gaelic stock.

Against this unsettled backdrop, Dermot MacMurrough, King of Leinster, scandalously abducted the not entirely unwilling wife of a rival King, thereby initiating a chain of events that was to change the course of Irish history. The outraged husband, Tiernan O' Rourke, joined forces with the High King of the time against MacMurrough, who, in the face of such

Kinsale

site of O'Neill's final defeat at the hands of the English

opposition, fled to Henry II of England to rally support. Henry's immediate concerns, however, lay elsewhere and on his advice, MacMurrough eventually secured the backing of "Strongbow", the adventuring and unprincipled Earl of Pembroke, under whose command the Anglo-Normans invaded Ireland in 1170, ostensibly to act as MacMurrough's protagonists.

The Anglo-Normans, themselves of Viking descent, were vastly superior militarily and soon controlled nearly all of Ireland bar the west and central Ulster. Making the most of a good opportunity they seized what land they could, consolidating their positions with great stone castles and rapidly forgetting their nominal allegiance to the English King. Strongbow meanwhile had married MacMurrough's daughter and succeeded as the powerful King of Leinster, exacerbating a situation which was far from ideal in Henry's eyes. Deeply unimpressed by the entire Irish scenario, in 1171 he invoked the support of the Pope, by happy coincidence an Englishman, and having been declared Lord of Ireland, arrived in person to assert his authority over both the Irish leaders and his recalcitrant Norman barons.

Henry landed at Waterford with a large naval force and declared the town a royal city. Under his overlordship, albeit in an absentee role, the prospect of English feudalism superseding the Gaelic tradition became a distinct possibility; however, such grass roots changes were not surprisingly violently resisted and although various Anglo-Norman administrative improvements were adopted, the Irish remained resolutely oblivious to any form of royal authority. In fact, over the following centuries the Anglo-Normans increasingly ignored their allegiance to the Crown, becoming "more Irish than the Irish", and entered into the fray of traditional Gaelic society to the extent that in 1366, an early Irish Parliament passed the Statutes of Kilkenny at the English king's behest to prevent any further assimilation. Intermarriage with the Irish was proscribed, the Irish were forbidden to enter walled cities and it became illegal to adopt Irish speech, dress or names. But it was too little too late. The process of integration was irreversible and by the sixteenth century the royal writ extended only to the Pale, a small area around Dublin beyond which anarchy reigned unchecked.

It was to this unsatisfactory state of affairs that Henry VIII addressed himself in the mid sixteenth century. When the powerful Fitzgeralds, Earls of Kildare and supposedly Crown representatives, openly rebelled against the monarchy, Henry was forced to act. In a series of deeply unpopular moves he declared himself head of the Irish Church and King of Ireland, attacked the property of the wealthy Catholic church and finally decreed that all lands, whether Irish or Anglo-Norman, be surrendered and regranted "by the grace of the King".

The plan was not fully implemented until Elizabeth I came to power and compounded the insult by ordering that the Irish be treated as savages to be subjugated and civilised using whatever brutal measures were deemed necessary. Two consequent Irish uprisings failed but the third, under the leadership of the powerful Ulsterman Hugh O'Neill was at least initially more successful. In 1598 he defeated an English army at Yellow Ford, and three years later a Spanish fleet landed at Kinsale in the south to support him. That O'Neill's army was in the north was, however, a disaster that culminated in defeat at English hands, and as a direct consequence the fall of Gaelic Ireland. O'Neill was forced to sign the Treaty of Mellifont in 1603 which handed authority over Ulster to the English, unaware that only days beforehand Elizabeth had died; apparently he wept with rage on hearing the news. Although his Gaelic loyalties had won the day, O'Neill had in his youth been a favourite of the English, the intention being to control Ulster through him, and to this end his lands were returned on the proviso that he pledge allegiance to the Crown. Thus resented by both sides, harassed by the Irish and despairing that he had become a pawn of the English, in 1607 he led the "Flight of the Earls", a mass exodus of Gaelic Chieftains who abandoned Ireland to the English and sailed to exile in Europe.

Ulster and much of Ireland was thus left leaderless and vulnerable to English control. Elizabeth had wisely chosen not to press her Protestantism on Ireland, fearing a retaliatory alliance with the foreign Catholic powers which would then have had a base uncomfortably close to the English coast. Nonetheless when she died, the staunchly Protestant James I inherited an Ireland in which a loathing of the English was already deeply rooted and which had only been coerced into some semblance of submission by a campaign of terror. From 1608 onwards, the English Government therefore systematically expropriated Irish land and "planted" it with Protestant English and Scottish settlers in an attempt to establish and consolidate the power of the Crown. The original plantation of Ulster, that most Catholic and Gaelic of provinces, was

undertaken by the Irish Society which consisted of Londoners and representatives of the City of London guilds prepared to fund the relocation of the planters. The best land of Ulster was divided between the various City companies and distributed amongst the settlers whilst the native Irish were evicted to the worst areas and charged extortionate rents for the privilege.

Although thousands of settlers did come, the geographical isolation of the Irish was never entirely achieved. It was often cheaper and easier to allow the Irish to stay in prohibited areas and charge them inflated rents than pay for planters to come over from England or Scotland. However, in contrast with previous invasions of Ireland, in which Celtic, Viking, and Anglo-Norman influences had been successively absorbed, in this case there was absolutely no cultural integration. The Protestant English were distinctly nervous at being surrounded by the furiously resentful Catholic Irish and the volatility of the situation was compounded when a second settlement of Ulster successfully introduced a thriving Scottish Presbyterian community to the province. The Presbyterians were persecuted by the Anglican (English Protestant) Church, completely at odds with the Catholics and resolutely determined to maintain their own religious interests. Under these unnatural and inauspicious circumstances, fear, bitterness and resentment were endemic and the disparate mix of race and religious beliefs sowed the seeds of the most vicious political instability.

In 1641 the inevitable happened and the Catholic Irish rose in rebellion against the planters. They were joined in a formal, if uneasy, alliance by the "Old" English, the Gaelicised Anglo-Normans, in return for Irish support for the restored Catholic English monarchy which was increasingly under threat from Cromwell's Protestant Puritans in England. The Rising was an uncontrolled outpouring of hatred which found expression in the most barbaric atrocities perpetrated against the Protestants. Although the scale of the horror was no doubt much exaggerated in the telling, it was nonetheless an episode that was to haunt the Protestant consciousness henceforth and feature frequently in anti-Catholic propaganda. Whatever the precise detail, the incontrovertible truth was that Ireland was already divided into two nations; Catholic and Protestant.

Retribution from England was delayed by the Civil War until Cromwell arrived in 1649. He embarked on a campaign to crush the English supporters of the Catholic monarchy and the Catholic Irish rebels with a ruthlessness that verged on the inhuman. Storming Drogheda, his army slaughtered the inhabitants with a lack of mercy that left, in his own words, "no priest alive", then marched victoriously south leaving a trail of inglorious devastation. By 1652, more than a quarter of the Irish Catholics had been massacred and many others sent to slavery in the West Indies. To add insult to injury, he decreed under the Act of Settlement

Oliver Cromwell

King of Independence
Tyrant of England

17th Century engraving

that the rebels' lands be confiscated and given to his English soldiers and financial backers. The dispossessed were banished to the infertile lands of Connacht - to hell or Connacht was an expression of the day - in a process which eventually reduced Irish landholdings from 59% in 1641 to 14% in 1695.

In 1660 Irish morale was raised by the Restoration of the Catholic Charles II to the English throne. Despite his lack of political acumen, he was, to the disappointment of the Irish, just astute enough not to alienate the Protestants who had secured him the crown after Cromwell's death. His successor, James II, seemed a better prospect, and indeed under his influence the Irish lot improved and Catholics soon dominated the political scene in Ireland. But this situation struck a less than comforting chord with the English Protestants, and when James passed an Act of Parliament decreeing religious tolerance for all denominations the English invited the Dutch and Protestant William of Orange, his son in law, to take over the throne. This was a cruel blow for the Irish, who had been eagerly awaiting the return of their lands under his repeal of Cromwell's Act of Settlement.

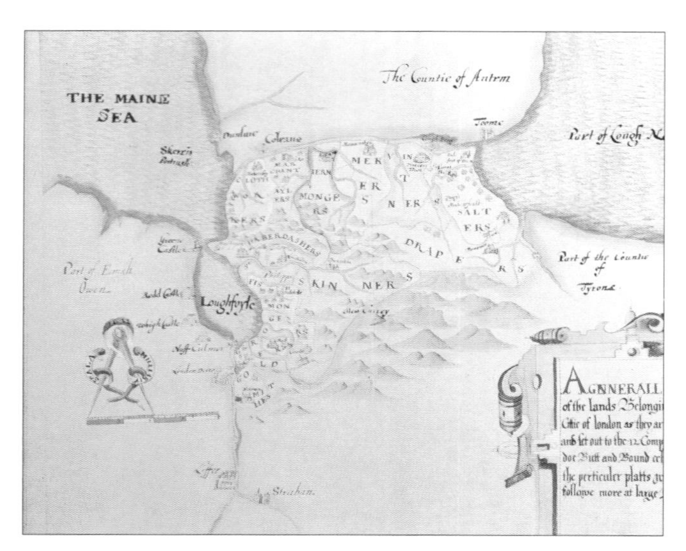

Plan of Londonderry
from Sir Thomas Phillips'
Survey of Londonderry
1622

James fled to France and thence to Ireland where he rallied his Catholic supporters and set about gaining control of Londonderry, one of only two Protestant garrisons left in the country. But rumours were rife of another Catholic Rising, memories of the previous bloodbath still fresh in Protestant minds, and thus it was that thirteen apprentices stole the keys of Londonderry and slammed the gates shut to James on the 7th December 1688 in an incident still commemorated in the Orange Day marches. The town was besieged and facing ruin; Lundy, given charge of the garrison, favoured surrender, but the disgust of the townspeople at this proposal forced him to escape in disguise and resulted in the term "Lundy" being coined in Northern Ireland for a Protestant whose resolve has weakened. Protestant troops twice arrived to help the beleaguered town, whose folk were reduced to eating mice and leather, but it was not until 1689 that British forces finally broke through and relieved the siege. Arguably, Londonderry may have been on the verge of surrender, but the fact that the town had not given in became a cornerstone of Protestant history and the basis of the slogan "No Surrender" which is still to be seen daubed throughout Northern Ireland.

In 1690, William of Orange landed at Carrickfergus Castle and won two resounding victories over the Catholics at the Battles of the Boyne and Aughrim, after which James abandoned all hope of regaining his crown and left for Europe. The following year, following the siege of Limerick, the Catholics finally also admitted defeat and bowed to the Treaty of Limerick, under which reasonably favourable provisions to protect their future status were laid down. In the event, quite the reverse happened; the terms were almost completely ignored and the Protestants were subsequently given the authority to control and marginalise the Catholics under the aegis of the Penal Laws, which formed a tranche of deeply discriminatory legislation aimed at annihilating both the spirit and the culture of the Catholic Irish. Among other restrictions, Catholics were prevented from entering public office, barred from parliamentary representation or professional employment, forbidden to educate their children in the Catholic faith, and prohibited from buying land. What property a landowner did possess was compulsorily divided on his death between his sons unless one converted to Protestantism, in which case the entire holding passed to him, with the result that by the start of the eighteenth century the Catholics, who represented about 80% of the population, owned less than 10% of Ireland.

Carrickfergus Castle

Thomas Creswick
(1811 - 69)

Although Catholicism itself was not specifically banned, the Penal Laws attacked the Church at the core by, amongst other things, outlawing bishops, archbishops and friars and thus making it theoretically impossible to ordain new priests. But given the deep rooted nature of Catholicism in Ireland, such laws were unenforcable in their entirety and so a modus operandi developed in which the Church was not quite as rigorously suppressed as it might have been, and as a focus for the dispossessed in fact grew ever stronger and more robust.

It was, however, not only the Catholics who suffered at the hands of the Protestants. Presbyterians were similarly persecuted, although to a lesser extent, and many emigrated to the Americas to escape both the Penal Laws and the cruelly disadvantageous restrictions which the English had imposed on Irish trade. As the eighteenth century progressed most Catholics were reduced to abject poverty and wretchedness, the unacceptable alternative being to convert to Protestantism to preserve their careers and property. Throughout the disempowered and embittered peasantry, secret agrarian societies formed to protect the tenants by administering rough and invariably brutal justice to the much vilified Protestant landowners, and indeed to those Catholics who were judged to deserve it. Sporting names such as the Whiteboys and the Molly Maguires, these societies made no pretence of political aspirations, despite wielding considerable local power.

Meanwhile, the elite landowning Protestant "Ascendancy" became wealthier, more powerful and, significantly, more discontented with the swingeing commercial restraints emanating from England. By the latter half of the eighteenth century, Georgian Dublin was Europe's fifth largest city, the Ascendancy was prosperous and confident, Ireland was scattered with elegant and extravagant mansions and even the middle class Catholic merchants - Catholics were not barred from trade and some had diplomatically declared allegiance to the Crown - were thriving. Subserviance to the British seemed increasingly unpalatable and so it was that

View of a House in Ireland *William Ashford (1746 - 1824)*

the Protestants voiced ever more pressing demands for Ireland to be recognised as an independent nation with an autonomous Parliament; sentiments that were further fuelled by the example of the American War of Independence in 1775 and the recognition that so many of the American rebels were Irish expatriots.

Added to the festering discontent in Ireland was the fact that the country was almost devoid of British troops due to the war in America, and had assembled a Protestant Volunteer force which numbered 80,000 by 1782 as a precaution against the threat of a French invasion. Britain was thus persuaded that it would be politic to listen to the eloquent and persuasive Henry Grattan, leader of the Patriot Party, who, his hand considerably strengthened by the veiled threat of the Volunteers, finally secured "complete legislative freedom" for the Irish Parliament in 1782. This terminology was at best an exaggeration and in reality virtually untrue in that real power was still vested in the honours and patronage decided in London, but it was nonetheless a step in the right direction. Grattan's Parliament, as it became known, was an entirely Protestant affair and despite the best intentions transpired to be woefully ineffectual. Grattan himself strongly believed in Catholic emancipation but for this, as for the reforms so necessary to give the Irish Parliament any real power, he had only patchy and inconsistent support. The plight of the Catholics remained desperate and although many of the Penal Laws were relaxed, the likelihood of the Irish effecting their own redemption seemed remote beyond belief.

However, in 1789 the foundations of the entire European establishment were totally undermined by the French Revolution. Peasant power was a new phenomenon and the complacency of a society hitherto secure in the invincibility of its position was shaken to the core. Inspired by the events in France and intoxicated by the cry of liberty, equality and fraternity, the Presbyterians of Belfast founded the Society of United Irishmen in a brave attempt to unite Catholic and Protestant, open the Irish Parliament to all creeds, and fight, albeit non-violently, for a truly independent Ireland. The term the Irish Republic was coined in the society as a direct result of the French revolution and under the leadership of Theobald Wolfe Tone, a Protestant Dubliner, the influence of the United Irishmen, radical but above ground, spread rapidly throughout Ireland.

By 1793 England was at war with the Republic of France and William Pitt, Prime Minister of England, fearing an alliance between the French and the Irish outlawed all radical societies. Tone fled temporarily to America whilst in his absence the United Irishmen, which by this stage had attracted a strong Catholic

Wolf Tone

The Great Court Yard, Dublin Castle 1792

James Malton (1761 - 1803)

following, became an underground secret society, intent on achieving its aims at whatever cost. Pitt was not far off the mark in predicting an alliance with the French, and in December 1796 at Tone's behest a large French fleet arrived at Bantry Bay to support the United Irishmen. Atrocious weather, which later became known as the 'Protestant Wind', prevented the ships from landing and a major crisis for the British was averted ; as Tone observed, "England had not such an escape since the Armada."

It was at this juncture the British Parliament finally took note of the situation and set about stamping out all sedition with a terrifying regime of torture and cruelty. Ruthless martial law soon broke the backbone of the United Irishmen in Ulster, helped significantly by the fact that many Protestants had reverted to their sectarian ways by joining the Orange Order, a movement with Masonic overtones which had evolved from a Protestant secret society in 1795. Elsewhere, Lord Edward Fitzgerald was plotting a countrywide rebellion, drawing support from the National Directory of United Irishmen which he had himself compiled. However the plan was poorly conceived, badly coordinated and ultimately devastated by informers. Nearly all the members of the National Directory were arrested and information about the society was extracted from the population with the utmost brutality, generating a wave of terror that swept through the country and culminated in May 1798 with the Great Rebellion. Six weeks later some 50,000 had died, the majority cut down in cold blood, and in a scenario that has become sadly familiar, atrocity led to and compounded counter atrocity. Thereafter, two more failed attempts at invasion by the French and the arrest and suicide of Wolfe Tone led to the total disintegration of the United Irishmen and their ideals. Ireland was emphatically not united and in fact sectarian attitudes had been exacerbated by the treatment meted out by Protestant to Catholic and Catholic to Protestant.

The result of this abortive Irish bid for independence was that an exasperated William Pitt proposed the abolition of the Irish Parliament and union with Britain. Although the Protestants were for the most part content to join forces with Britain, discomfited as they were by the situation in Ireland, the will to abolish the Irish Parliament and thereby remove much of their own power was significantly encouraged by bribes of titles and offices of state, hence many Irish earldoms date from this period. Within a year of its proposal, 5 to 1 against had become a majority in favour of union and thus the Irish Parliament voted itself out of existence and Ireland became constitutionally joined with Great Britain on 1 January 1801. Although some of the wealthier Catholics were also in favour of union on the grounds that Pitt had promised to repeal those Penal Laws which had not been removed in 1793, the majority assumed the nationalist stance originally the domain of the Protestants. Independence seemed an impossible goal, despite a last ditch attempt by the well-intentioned if misguided Robert Emmett, whose plan to seize the seat of British power in Dublin went badly awry and gave rise to his famous last words, "Let no man write my epitaph ... when my country takes her place among the nations of the earth, then and not till then let my epitaph be written."

Dublin Castle *the main entrance*

Pitt was genuinely in favour of Catholic emancipation, but he was soon ousted from power and thus it was left to Daniel O'Connell, the "Liberator" (from Protestant oppression rather than British rule), to achieve the right to sit in Parliament and hold public office for his fellow countrymen. O'Connell had been educated in France and his deeply entrenched opposition to the use of violence sprang from an early exposure to the brutal methods of the French army. The Catholic Association he founded in 1823 with the wholehearted support of the Catholic Church was therefore a peaceful, although large and powerful, organisation whose potential for violence was kept in check by him alone - a fact of which he was not entirely averse to apprising the British.

O'Connell's first major achievement was in fact a double victory; in the 1826 General Election he engineered the election of a pro-emancipation Protestant candidate with the overwhelming backing of the Association; previously it would have been unthinkable for any but anti-emancipation candidates even to be allowed to stand. Inspired by the scale of his success, two years later O'Connell himself stood for a seat in County Clare and was voted into power with an enormous majority, thanks again to his well disciplined supporters. That Catholics were still proscribed from sitting in Parliament was, however, a political conundrum for the British; they were fully aware of the dangers of alienating the sleeping giant Association and this, in conjunction with the pro-emancipation sympathies of many British MPs, eventually forced the Government to accept the inevitable and pass the Emancipation Act in 1829. It was an enormous moral victory for the Catholic Irish, who, for the first time, were granted the right to be elected as MPs and take part in the political scene.

Ten years later O'Connell used the same peaceful tactics - reinforced once more by the unspoken threat of the Association in the background - to try and overturn the Act of Union and restore an Irish Parliament, which, unlike Grattan's, would admit Catholics as well as Protestants. By 1843 his popularity in Ireland was phenomenal, and 'monster meetings' such as that held symbolically on the Royal Hill of Tara attracted over a million supporters. Still advocating pacifism, O'Connell's movement generated great sympathy worldwide, but it was his profound belief that "no political change is worth the shedding of a single drop of human blood" that was ultimately his downfall. Putting this assertion to the test, the British decreed a meeting planned for Clontarf illegal and, to the dismay of his followers, O'Connell stepped down in accordance with his principles and played no further part in Irish politics.

Although repeal of the union was still a long way off, O'Connell's gift of political power to the Irish was a spectacular achievement. Any political aspirations were, however, almost immediately overshadowed by the Great Famine which for four wretched years devastated Ireland. The introduction of the easily grown and nutritious potato and the lowering of the marriage age had helped double the population of Ireland between 1800 and 1840 to eight million, resulting in the subdivision of individual land holdings into the tiniest of plots. As the vast majority of the impoverished peasantry subsisted entirely on potatoes, the tragic

Irish Emigrants
John Joseph Barker
(1824 - 1904)

consequences of the potato crop of 1845 falling victim to a lethal blight were terrifyingly apparent. Bad weather and three more years of failed crops reduced the Irish population by over two million. Almost half of these died in truly horrifying circumstances, starving to death and dying of disease in the most degrading and appalling conditions - mothers reduced to eating the flesh of their dead children were not unheard of. The other million plus escaped the purgatory by emigrating to America or Canada on what became known as coffin ships, so low were the expectations of arriving alive at the destination.

Ireland's other crops, unaffected by blight, remained beyond the reach of the desperate peasantry who were unable to afford even the subsidised maize which the British Government eventually and belatedly provided. Rent took priority and many absentee

Kilmainham Gaol
built in 1863, now a museum

English landlords, operating through a chain of avaricious middle men, evicted destitute tenants with a chilling lack of compassion. There were of course many exceptions, but the succour of the Irish people undoubtedly lay in the hands of the British Government, which remained rigid in its belief that excessive intervention would merely interfere with the natural processes of free trade and private enterprise and foster a permanent dependence on the state. As a result what measures the Government did take were piteously inadequate and Britain's perceived neglect of Ireland's suffering bequeathed to the Irish people a bitterness that is still extant. By 1847 a quarter of a million Irish were emigrating annually, setting up distinct Catholic Irish communities in the New World, and carrying with them a legacy of hatred for the British which rapidly evolved into political activity.

Meanwhile in Ireland the Young Irelanders had come into being. Believing implicitly in Ireland's historical right to independence, they were politically inept and shunned by the influential Church for espousing the use of violence; in their eyes O'Connell's pacifist approach had been a failure. In 1848 they were involved in a farcical clash with the Irish Constabulary which, despite the portentous title of "The Rising of "48", was more realistically represented as the less glamourous "Battle of Widow MacCormack's cabbage garden." The Young Irelanders were sent packing and one of their number, James Stephens, escaped to Paris where, impressed by the secret societies there, he concluded that organisation and professionalism, qualities thus far conspicuously lacking in the cause for independence, were of paramount importance.

Stephens was a man of prodigious energy and confidence and in 1856 he set about assessing the situation in Ireland personally and on foot. Undeterred by the fact that the general mood in Ireland verged more towards the disaffected than the overtly revolutionary, he founded what was later to be known as the Irish Republican Brotherhood (IRB) with the promise "to renounce all allegiance to the Queen of England ... and fight ... to make Ireland an Independent Democratic Republic." He then went to America to establish a sister society, the Fenian Brotherhood, named romantically, if inaccurately it was to transpire, after an ancient warrior elite. Stephens was well aware of the benefits of secrecy after the debacle of the United Irishmen, and the IRB was therefore run on intensely secret lines and generally referred to in Ireland under its American counterpart's name. By 1865 Stephens was promising action within the year, counting on 85,000 men in Ireland and hoping for support from America. However, Irish American backing in terms of men and supplies was not as forthcoming as had been expected, and betrayals, informants and deferred plans combined to sabotage further the action of the Fenians, whose military ineptitude and a debilitating lack of leadership eventually reduced the entire campaign to little more than a disastrous fiasco.

By the end of the 1870s famine threatened Ireland again. Although a crisis was averted, failing potato crops combined with cheap American grain imports initiated an all too familiar wave of evictions for those tenants unable to pay their rent. In 1879 Michael Davitt, whose parents had been evicted from their land in the 1850s, established the Land League to agitate for reduced rents, fixity of tenure and ultimately the transfer of land ownership to tenants. To help lead his cause he enrolled Charles Parnell, the passionate and aggressive MP for Meath who, despite being a wealthy Protestant landowner himself, came from a background which espoused Irish independence and had little sense of obligation to Britain.

The resulting Land War, which lasted until 1882, was a violent affair. Although the public stance of the Land League was pacifist, many members hailed from the secret agrarian societies and were accustomed to adopting a forceful approach to their problems. They were hardly discouraged by the official dictates of the Land League's leaders, couched as they were in such vague terms as, "shooting landlords is wrong because the assailant frequently misses and hits someone else." For his part, Parnell was careful to be seen to be unaware of the unsavoury practices employed and advocated instead the tactic of boycotting, so named after a Captain Boycott who attempted to take over an evicted tenant's land and was thereafter condemned to complete ostracism.

As the unrest in Ireland escalated, Gladstone, the newly elected Liberal Prime Minister of Britain, introduced the Land Act of 1881 in recognition of the exigency of the situation. This bestowed enormous benefits on the tenants in that fair rents were introduced and the possibility of land ownership was raised, but it was not enough for Parnell who, by this stage leader of the Irish Party, had the financially indispensable but independence minded Americans and Fenians of Ireland to answer to.

Thus trapped by extremists, his increasingly belligerent and provocative speeches eventually led to arrest and imprisonment. He was freed on the understanding that in return for consideration of the outstanding land matters and, hopefully, the nationalist question, he would bring the ever more wayward Land League into line. The Chief Secretary of Ireland resigned in disgust over this and was replaced by Gladstone's nephew, Lord Cavendish, who was barbarically murdered in Phoenix Park on the very night of his arrival in Dublin.

This soured relations between Parnell and Gladstone considerably, but nonetheless Gladstone was sympathetic to Parnell's uncompromising campaign for Home Rule. Additionally, Parnell's control of the majority of Irish seats in Parliament was essential for Gladstone's balance of power over the Conservatives. In spite of such apparent support, in the first Home Rule Bill was defeated in the Commons in 1886 for several reasons. Most Conservatives believed that Home Rule, ie Irish legislature over domestic affairs, was but a stepping stone towards full constitutional independence, whilst the powerful Protestants of Ulster, enjoying the benefits of the industrial revolution and trade relations with Britain, were appalled at the possible commercial implications, to the extent that Anglican and Presbyterian united in vehement opposition to the Bill. And given the deeply ingrained Protestant opposition to any form of Catholic power, it was in all a formidable force that opposed the prospect of Home Rule.

By 1889 Parnell was at the height of his political career. His fall from grace was therefore all the more spectacular when the husband of Katharine O'Shea, his long-standing mistress, cited him in divorce proceedings and revealed the more sordid details of their passionate affair. Shunned by the horrified Catholics of Ireland and similarly rejected by Victorian England, he fought desperately to regain his stature but to no avail. He was deposed as leader of the Irish Party, which was riven into pro and anti-Parnell factions. The problem of Home Rule was temporarily eclipsed by the scandal and, having married Kitty, he died less than a year later in 1891.

The following year, the Liberals returned to government with a large enough majority to see the Home Rule Bill through the Commons despite concerted opposition from the Conservatives and Ulster Protestants; "playing the Orange card" was Lord Randolph Churchill's description of the alliance the Conservatives had forged with the Protestant "Unionists". In the event, it was the House of Lords which vetoed the Bill for the second time, but nonetheless it was abundantly clear that Home Rule was a distinct possibility for the future. It was not, however, for nearly twenty years that the issue arose again. Although far reaching land reforms and vast increases in tenant landholdings had overshadowed the question of nationalism in the interim, a Gaelic revival had done much to restore Irish pride and resulted in the formation of the Gaelic League, an Irish literary movement, the Gaelic Athletics Association and in general the rejuvenation of traditional Gaelic culture. As part of this cultural renaissance, in the final years of the nineteenth century Arthur Griffith had advocated the formation of a separate Parliament for Ireland to be based in Dublin under the banner of Sinn Fein, meaning "We, ourselves" or "Ourselves, Alone."

In 1910, the Liberals were back in power, and their majority over the Conservatives was slight enough for Irish support again to be vital. Important enough certainly to warrant trading a Home Rule Bill for the support of the Irish Nationalist Party MPs. The House of Lords had been stripped of its power of veto and thus the Bill, which was introduced in 1912, seemed virtually certain to become law. Determined at all costs to avoid such a contingency, the leader of the Protestant Ulster Unionists, the formidable lawyer Sir Edward Carson declared that should this "most nefarious conspiracy" result in Home Rule, the Unionists would immediately set up their own Parliament in Ulster. Nearly half a million Protestants signed a "Solemn League and Covenant", many of them in their own blood, opposing Home Rule or at the least petitioning for the exclusion of Ulster. To reinforce the Unionist position, the Ulster Volunteer Force was formed in 1913, organised through the Orange Lodges, and by the following year had accrued a significant stash of arms. Not only were the Unionists thus armed and prepared to fight for their cause, but they also had the backing of the Conservatives; in the words of the Conservative leader, there was "no length of resistance to which Ulster will go in which I shall not support them".

Carson did eventually propose a compromise in which only the six most Protestant of the nine counties of Ulster should be excluded from Home Rule and this conciliatory gesture considerably weakened the Liberals' opposition to the total exclusion of the North from the Bill. The Irish Nationalist Party, under the leadership of John Redmond, was, however, horrified by the prospect of a divided Ireland; "the two nation theory is to us an abomination and a blasphemy" were his unequivocal words on the subject. To counterbalance the Ulster Volunteer Force, the pro-full Home Rule supporters in the south of Ireland formed the Irish Volunteers, but they were far less well equipped and organised than their Protestant counterparts. Redmond had finally acquiesced to the exclusion argument and offered any Ulster county the option to remain out of a Dublin Parliament indefinitely when, at this crucial juncture, the outbreak of World War I brought the negotiating process abruptly to a halt and diverted all attention away from domestic matters.

The Bill was rapidly pushed through Parliament with, on one hand, the agreement of Carson and the Conservatives to defer their insistence on an Amending Bill to deal with Ulster, and, on the other, the understanding with Redmond that Home Rule be suspended for 12 months or the duration of the war, whichever proved longer. As a result Redmond pledged the support of the Irish Volunteers for the British war effort on an unspoken quid pro quo basis for Home Rule once the war was over. What he had inexplicably overlooked though was the absolute resistance of the Protestants to a Dublin Parliament. They had, after all, made it perfectly clear that under no circumstances was government from the south even remotely acceptable.

Redmond's supporters were not unanimously convinced of British resolve regarding Home Rule and a radical breakaway group of extremists separated from the Irish Volunteers, retaining the name, whilst the remainder assumed the title of the National Volunteers. Under Patrick Pearse, a schoolmaster who held an almost spiritual belief in the need for blood to be spilled for the Irish cause, the new Irish Volunteers teamed up with the Citizens' Army, founded by the workers' champion and ardent Republican, James Connolly, and the rejuvenated Irish Republican Brotherhood. A general agreement was reached to rebel against the British Government before the war was over, but it was Pearse and Connolly who actually put the plan into practice, planning a secret Rising for Easter Sunday 1916, with arms to be supplied from Germany.

So secret in fact were the plans that even Eoin MacNeill, official leader of the Volunteers, was unaware of what was going on until the last minute. Believing in violence only as a final resort, he refused to sanction the Rising and to that effect placed an advertisement in the newspaper cancelling the "manoeuvres" planned for Sunday. Given that most of the rank and file to be involved were completely unaware of the real intention, this greatly confused the situation and by the time Pearse and Connolly had mustered what support they could in Dublin, the failure of the rebellion was a foregone conclusion. Nonetheless on Easter Monday, to the embarrassment of the British Army which was caught unawares and the bemusement of the populace of Dublin, around 800 armed Republicans marched into the city and established a headquarters in the General Post Office, whence, to the astonishment of the baffled onlookers, Pearse proclaimed in rousing tones that Ireland was henceforward a Republic, supported by her gallant ally Germany.

Sackville Street, Dublin

showing the Post Office and Nelson's Column

Samuel Frederick Brocas (1792 - 1847)

The rebels held out for nearly a week against the British Army, during which time the centre of Dublin was reduced to ruins and more than 200 civilians were killed. Once they had surrendered, the Republicans had to be protected by the British, so unpopular were they with the Dubliners for causing such damage to their beautiful city and such a wanton waste of life. The punishment meted out by the British was, initially, surprisingly lenient, especially given the rebels' professed alliance with the Government's enemy in a time of war, and had the British Government taken heed of the words of one Irish MP who wrote to Redmond, "Do not fail to urge the Government not to execute any of the prisoners", the Easter Rising would probably have faded into insignificance. As it was, the British attitude changed and execution after execution was carried out, making martyrs of the leaders and prompting a violent backlash reaction in Ireland. With the news that James Connolly, the fifteenth and final victim, had been shot tied to a chair as he was unable to stand came a transformation in Irish sympathies. The Republican cause was made and, as one leader predicted, "Between this moment and freedom, Ireland will go through hell."

During his imprisonment after the Rising, Michael Collins, a member of the IRB, began to coordinate a network of IRB and Volunteer contacts throughout Ireland, whilst simultaneously identifying those members of the Royal Irish Constabulary (the main instrument of British power in Ireland) who were sympathetic to the cause - contacts that were to prove vital in the future. Once released he set about swaying public opinion in favour of Republicanism; in conjunction with the supporters of Sinn Fein, he put up trophy

Republican candidates for two bye-elections whose sensational victories over the Nationalist Parliamentary Party candidates helped generate a general mood swing in support of the cause. Eamon de Valera, one of the few surviving leaders of the Easter Rising, whose death sentence had been commuted due to his US citizenship, was the third Republican to win an election with a landslide victory and it was he who gained the crucial support of the Catholic clergy.

Under his leadership, the various Republican factions were united under the umbrella of Sinn Fein which, although clear in its goal of achieving independent Republic status for Ireland, was otherwise somewhat vague on its policies. Support for the party, which was initially less than widespread, increased dramatically when the British Government mooted the idea of conscription in Ireland after suffering devastating losses in the trenches of France. In the face of massive opposition the plan was rapidly abandoned, but the damage had been done and Sinn Fein reaped enormous benefits from the hostility the Government had engendered. In the first General Election after the war ended in 1918 the vast majority of Irish seats were won by Sinn Fein. It was a resounding victory over the Nationalist Party, which was all but obliterated, and one to which several factors other than an explosion in Republican feeling had contributed. Not least of these were the carefully planned and extensive poll rigging which involved some voters voting up to twenty times and the fact that most soldiers in the Army, who would probably have voted otherwise, were still away from home.

Having been elected, the new Sinn Fein MPs refused to take up their seats at Westminster and instead set up a Parliament, the Dail Eireann, in Dublin from where they declared Ireland to be a sovereign independent Republic. The British Government, adopting the attitude that to declare independence was a far cry from attaining it, ignored the situation and the Irish, hoping for recognition from the American President, Woodrow Wilson, as an independent nation were further thwarted by his reluctance to sour relations with Britain after the shared victory in the war. Matters were not improved even when de Valera went to New York in 1919 to rally support and returned, despite having been much feted and with a considerable injection of funds, without the longed for official recognition of Ireland as a Republic.

Peaceable tactics seemed to be failing for Sinn Fein and although de Valera had specifically forbidden the use of violence, two members of the Royal Irish Constabulary (RIC) were shot, without authorisation, on the day the Dail convened for the first time. It was the first of a series of killings which the militant Michael Collins subsequently masterminded in a bloody campaign against the British which was to last for two and a half years.

Collins, who was a magnetic and charismatic personality and a consummate organiser, initially directed the campaign at members of the RIC whom he identified through his contacts as being unsympathetic to the Republican cause. By the end of 1919 fourteen police had been killed and more wounded by his force of Volunteers, which soon became known as the Irish Republican Army (IRA).

Retaliation came in the form of the infamous "Black and Tans", British reinforcements for the RIC who were equipped with mismatching khaki and green uniforms and thus acquired their sobriquet after a pack of hounds in County Tipperary where they were first deployed. The new recruits were tough and brutal and soon earned a well deserved and enduring reputation for viciousness. They were augmented by an elite force of British ex-army officers,

Government buildings *Merrion Street, Dublin*

the Auxiliaries, who constituted an aggressive and formidable weapon against the IRA. Guerrilla warfare became rife between the two sides and public opinion swung ever further from the British as the people of Ireland, caught in the crossfire, witnessed the tactics of the easily identified British contingent. Not, indeed, that the IRA were any less ruthless: "Spy killed by IRA" was the blunt message frequently to be found pinned to Irish corpses, police and civilian informers were dispatched with impunity, and terrorist atrocities destroyed much of the infrastructure of Ireland. In a war in which there were no rules, posters nailed to the trees by the RIC stating that for every member of the Crown forces shot, two Sinn Feiners would die were a terrifying indication of the level to which the conflict had degenerated.

In an attempt to defuse the situation, the British Government passed the Government of Ireland Act in 1920, creating separate parliaments for 'Northern Ireland' and the twenty six counties of 'Southern Ireland'. It had little impact. The elections in the following year were treated by the members of the Dail Eireann as elections for the whole of Ireland and de Valera was declared President. The Ulster Protestants were equally determined not to give in and abandon the Union and against a background of escalating violence, in which horrific deeds were perpetrated by both sides, the urgency of finding a compromise became ever more apparent.

In July 1921, a truce was agreed between the British and de Valera and the following December, after protracted and intensely difficult negotiations, the Anglo-Irish Treaty was signed in London by Lloyd George and an Irish delegation headed by Michael Collins and Arthur Griffith. Although the Treaty gave the nationalists more than they could have expected with Home Rule, in that an Irish Free State was created with constitutional independence and dominion status on a par with that of Canada, there were two insurmountable stumbling blocks as far as the Republicans were concerned. First, there was the abhorrent issue of allegiance to the British Crown - the Free State was emphatically not a Republic - and secondly, Ireland had been effectively partitioned when the six largely Protestant counties of the North had been allowed to opt out of the Free State a month after the Treaty came into being.

De Valera, who, despite being head of the Government, had not been consulted in the final hectic stages of negotiations with the British, was determined not to compromise his Republican stance and, adamantly rejecting the Treaty, resigned as President. Collins on the other hand, although acknowledging that it was far from ideal, took the view that it was a "chance for freedom to achieve freedom". He had also been persuaded to accept the unpalatable prospect of partition on the grounds that a Boundary Commission set up within the terms of the Treaty to adjust the borders of the North would reduce the area to be excluded from the Free State to such an extent that it would cease to be a viable entity. The IRA was more or less evenly split in its loyalties between the two points of view and Ireland rapidly divided into pro- and anti-Treaty factions. After twelve days of vitriolic debate, the

Stormont

Dail ratified the Treaty in January 1922 by a tiny majority and the following June, in the first Irish Free State elections, the people of Ireland did the same.

Two weeks later Civil War broke out. The men who so recently had been fighting together against the Black and Tans now fought each other in what became known as the War of Brothers, a bitter and economically devastating conflict in which the depth of feeling was summarised by the Republican song:

"Take it down from the mast, Irish traitors, The flag we Republicans claim.
It can never belong to Free Staters, You've brought on it nothing but shame."

Collins' talents for organisation again came to the fore and he marshalled the pro-Treaty IRA into an efficient Free State Army, armed in part with British weapons, whilst the anti-Treaty IRA set about achieving their aim of a free and united Republic of Ireland with guerrilla tactics that soon earned them the nickname of "irregulars".

In August 1922, Arthur Griffith, who had been elected President after de Valera resigned in high dudgeon, collapsed from exhaustion and died of a heart attack. Collins met his death at the hands of anti-Treaty Republicans in his native County Cork at the same time and in their absence, the Free State Government passed the Emergency Powers Bill under which any Republican in arms was to be executed unless he surrendered. In the 7 months from November 1922, 77 Republicans were executed, including Erskine Childers who was found in possession of a small revolver and whose death provoked a backlash decree from the Republicans that any member of the Dail who had voted for the Emergency Powers Bill be shot on sight.

By the following May the military effectiveness of the IRA had been severely reduced and after the 77th Republican execution, de Valera called for his followers to lay down their arms with the assurance that "other means must be sought to safeguard the nation's rights". After a year in jail, he refused to take his place in the Dail because to do so he was required to swear an oath of allegiance, and thus both military and democratic resistance to the Free State came to lie in abeyance. In 1925, with the agreement of the leaders of the Free State Government, the Boundary Commission was abolished in return for the removal of various financial obligations to the British. With its abolition died any short term likelihood of reuniting Ireland and thus the seal was put on the partition of the country into two parts, the Free State, which became the Republic of Ireland, and Northern Ireland.

De Valera boycotted the Dail for four years until 1927 when he formed Fianna Fail (the Warriors of Ireland), which maintained his anti-Treaty standpoint, and which came to power in 1932. Five years later he introduced a new constitution abolishing the oath of allegiance to the British crown, claiming sovereignty over the six counties of the North and renaming the Irish Free State "Eire", to be governed by a two chamber Parliament in which the Prime Minister was called the Taoiseach. Fianna Fail remained in power for sixteen years until 1949 when Fine Gael (the Tribe of Ireland and directly descended from the first Free State Government) won the election and declared Eire to be a Republic - at last.

Northern Ireland remained part of the United Kingdom and retained a large degree of legislative autonomy exercised from Stormont in Belfast. However the province was, and still is, deeply divided on religious grounds and Protestant domination in virtually all aspects of life led to the formation of a Civil Rights movement in 1967 to campaign for fairer representation for Catholics. In 1969, violent rioting between Catholic and Protestants in Derry resulted in the British Army being called in as a peacekeeping force, marking the start of twenty five years of "troubles". Despite being welcomed initially by the Catholics, the Army was soon perceived to be allied with the Protestants in a conflict that was becoming increasingly vicious, and within months the quiescent IRA joined forces with the Catholic community and mounted a campaign of terror which soon spread from Northern Ireland to mainland Britain. In 1972 the Northern Ireland Parliament was abolished after the death on "Bloody Sunday" of 13 civilians shot by British troops, in retaliation for which the British Embassy in Dublin was attacked and burnt. The following year, at Sunningdale, a power sharing arrangement to represent both Unionists and Nationalists was formulated and in November 1973 an elected executive took office. It was, however, a short lived exercise, rejected overwhelmingly by the Unionist Protestants of Northern Ireland, and after a crippling general strike by the largely Protestant Ulster Workers Union, government reverted to Westminster.

Given that the ambition of the Republic of Ireland and the IRA is to reunite the North with the Republic, and given the fierce resistance to such an eventuality by the Unionists of the North, it is little wonder that the situation in Ireland is as difficult as it is. However, in the early nineties, moves for talks between the Dublin Government, the Northern Ireland political parties and the British Government were initiated as a result of which there is, finally, some hope of finding a lasting peace for this beautiful and troubled land.

Ireland today

Lashed by the storm-ridden Atlantic, washed by enshrouding clouds, Ireland's verdant landscape has, over the centuries, been witness to countless tales of atrocity and human suffering. Even today, the past is ever-present in a land where ancient wrongs retain powerful force.

And yet no country could be more welcoming to the foreign visitor. From its lively and joyous cities to the beguiling beauties of its rural areas, Ireland captivates its guests with a warmth and the special Irish charm for which it has become legendary.

The following pages take a closer look at Ireland region by region, examining principal points of interest and highlighting major events, and provide an insight into some of the natural and cultural forces which continue to define its distinctive character.

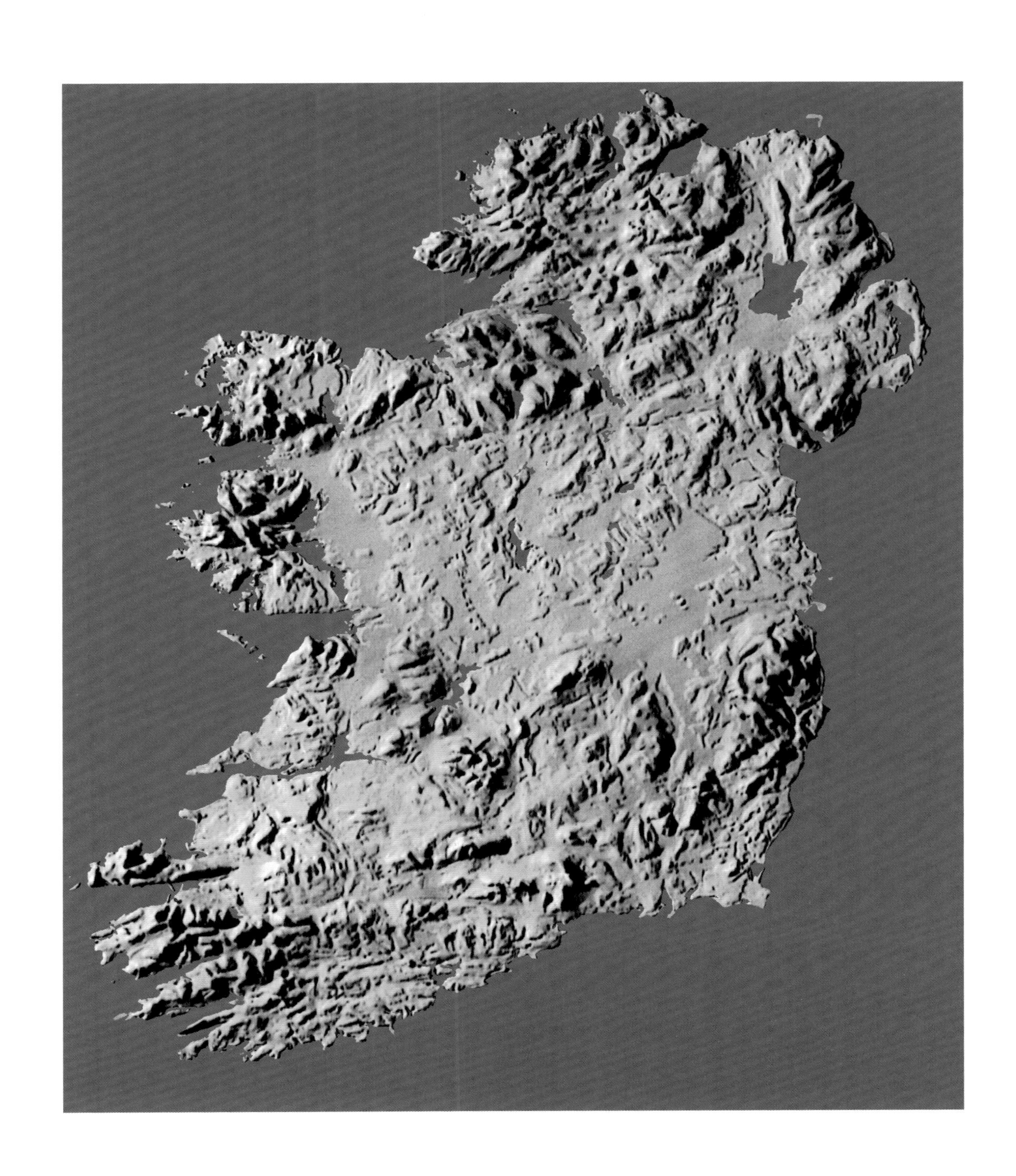

Dublin

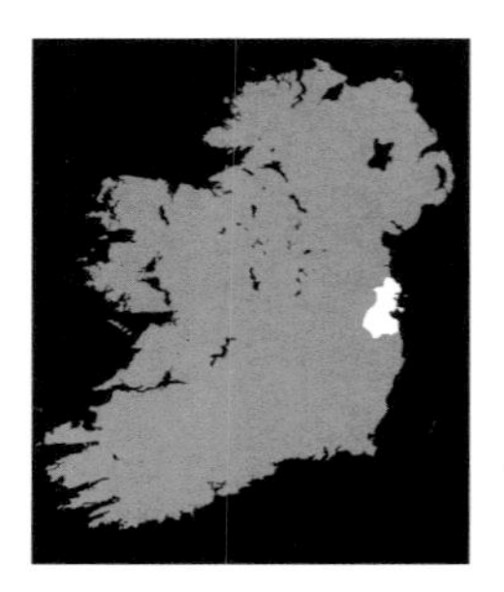

The beguiling city of Dublin has been the capital of the Republic of Ireland since independence in 1921 and as befits the capital of such a beautiful country lies in a spectacular setting, spread around the sweeping arc of Dublin Bay and framed by the backdrop of the Wicklow Mountains to the south. Imbued with a casual yet charming atmosphere, Dublin is a city of great contrasts; an outstanding literary heritage coexists with an unrivalled pub scene whilst eighteenth century Georgian splendour and elegance rest easily alongside an effervescent twentieth century culture.

Dublin, despite having somewhat arbitrarily celebrated its millennium in 1988, was first settled by the Celts on the banks of the River Liffey long before 988AD. Dublin's Gaelic name, Baile Atha Cliath, translates as the Bridge of the Hurdle Ford, where the royal road from Tara crossed the Liffey en route to Wicklow, and the earliest evidence of habitation is recorded on Ptolemy's map of 140AD as a settlement called Eblana. In the middle of the fifth century St Patrick arrived to convert the inhabitants to Christianity and although a Christian settlement subsequently developed around the ford, it was not until the ninth century, when the Vikings arrived in force, that anything resembling a town appeared. They established a raiding and trading base at the black pool where the now virtually defunct River Poddle and the Liffey met, thereby giving Dublin its modern name; black pool being rendered in Irish as dubh linn.

Although Brian Boru defeated the Danes at the battle of Clontarf in 1014, control of Dublin remained effectively in Viking hands until the advent of the Anglo-Normans in 1170, whose military prowess heralded not only the downfall of the Norsemen, but also the start of centuries of English occupation. Strongbow, the commander of the Anglo-Normans, rapidly built himself a considerable power base in Ireland, setting an example which was readily followed by his knights, who fortified their recently acquired holdings with the first stone castles to be found in the country. At this juncture the English King, Henry II, severely discomfited by the increasing power of his barons and their less than dutiful acknowledgement of him, came to Dublin to assert his authority over both the Irish and his wayward nobility. Thereafter Dublin became the capital of the area over which the English held sway, which was enclosed by a wooden palisade and thus became known as the Pale. The expression "beyond the Pale" arose as a direct result of the fact that beyond the palisade Crown authority stood for precisely nothing.

As the English Protestant Ascendancy flourished, so early eighteenth century Dublin flourished in tandem, entering a cultural heyday which left a spectacular legacy of furniture,

Custom House

The River Liffey and the Law Courts

J Huberts 1879

silver and architecture. Bridges were built over the Liffey and perfectly proportioned Georgian houses laid out in formal terraces and squares transformed Dublin from relative obscurity to the second largest city in the British Empire and one of Europe's architectural glories. The wealthy abandoned overcrowded mediaeval Dublin south of the Liffey for the planned elegance of Georgian Dublin to the north, in which the creation of gracious avenues was greatly assisted by the formation in 1757 of the practical, if somewhat bizarre, Commission for Making Wide and Convenient Streets. The poor followed in their footsteps and thus, ironically, fashionable society soon fled south again to the grandeur of Merrion Square, Fitzwilliam Square and the area surrounding St Stephen's Green to escape the slums which were rapidly burgeoning northwards.

At the same time, public building also boomed and architects such as James Gandon, Richard Cassels, or Castle, and Edward Lovett Pearce designed some of Dublin's most beautiful landmark buildings. What is now the grandiose Bank of Ireland was built by Lovett Pearce in the eighteenth century and housed Grattan's Parliament, the Protestant Ascendancy's short lived bid for independence of 1792. Sadly his optimistic pronouncement that "Ireland is now a nation" transpired to be little more than wishful thinking, and as the Irish Parliament voted itself out of existence with the Act of Union in 1801, so Dublin's fortunes collapsed and the city entered a period of sad decline.

In the early years of the twentieth century, Dublin became a focal point of Republican agitation for independence after the Easter Rising of 1916, during which parts of the city centre were reduced to ruins and the General Post Office, an attractive but otherwise unremarkable building in O'Connell Street, rose to fame as the headquarters of the rebels. In 1921, the stately eighteenth century Custom House was the target of an audacious but unsuccessful strike by the IRA at the heart of British administration in Ireland, the upshot of which was a truce between the British and the Irish which led ultimately to the Anglo-Irish Treaty of 1921 and the creation of the Irish Free State. The Treaty notwithstanding, Dublin's troubles were not yet over. In 1922 the Four Courts, another dignified building on the north bank of the Liffey, became the headquarters of the anti-Treaty Republicans (who viewed the agreement as a sell-out) and the subsequent shelling of the building by the pro-Treaty faction (who viewed it as a stepping stone in the right direction) was the flashpoint which provoked a year of devastating Civil War. Again Dublin suffered cruelly and much of the city's glorious and irreplaceable Georgian legacy was lost forever as a result.

Despite such a tragic and destructive catalogue of events, Dublin remains a beautiful city and in 1991 it was named European City of Culture. A recent renaissance and sensitive redevelopment have ensured that it retains the cosmopolitan appeal and irresistible charm that make it uniquely attractive among European capitals.

Many of Dublin's historical buildings lie south of the Liffey, amongst them Trinity College, which is officially the University of Dublin but is always referred to after its only college. Founded by Elizabeth I in 1592 in an attempt to prevent students from being "infected by Popery", a free education was initially offered to any Catholic prepared to convert to Protestantism. Catholics were, in fact, totally banned from Trinity until 1793, after which limited entrance was permitted, if only on pain of excommunication by the Catholic Church - a restriction which lasted in some form until 1970. Just after the turn of the twentieth century and significantly earlier than most Universities, Trinity admitted women in an act so violently opposed by the Provost of the time, George Salmon, that his immediate death was regarded less as a sad but natural occurrence than the obdurate fulfilment of a promise to admit women only over his dead body.

The chapel at Trinity is remarkable for its painted, rather than stained, glass windows, the largest of which commemorates Archbishop Ussher, a college founder, whose most extraordinary, not to mention confident, feat was to date the creation to exactly 4004 BC. However, it is the Old Library wherein lie Trinity's principal glories. Not only is Trinity a copyright library and thus entitled to a free copy of every book published in the UK and Ireland, a logistical nightmare which requires an additional kilometre of shelving every year to house the new editions, but it is also home to the priceless Book of Kells. This exquisite manuscript is one of the oldest books in the world and consists of 680 spectacularly decorated and illuminated pages. It was almost certainly produced by the monks on the Scottish Isle of Iona around 800 AD before being taken for safekeeping to the monastery of Kells in Ireland to escape the increasingly belligerent Vikings. No expense was spared in its creation; the most skilled illuminators were employed, parchment from hundreds of calf hides and rare and precious inks from as far afield as the Hindu Kush mountains were used to make the Book of Kells one of the greatest and most magnificent treasures of the world.

Just west of Trinity lies Temple Bar, an ancient area of Dublin, which was built on land wrested from the monasteries in Henry VIII's 1537 campaign against the Catholic Church. In the eighteenth century it became a focus for the less salubrious side of Dublin life; however, brothels and pubs notwithstanding, it was the site of the first performance of Handel's Messiah, conducted by Handel himself in the wonderfully named Fishamble Street in 1741.

To the south of Temple Bar Dublin Castle, a palatial affair where the Presidents of Ireland are inaugurated, was built on the site of an ancient Celtic fort at the behest of King John in 1204. From the reign of Elizabeth I onwards it was the official residence of the British Viceroys and remained the symbol of British power in Ireland until independence in 1921. As such, the contrast between the opulence of the interior and the poverty of the surrounding slums was profound and certainly deemed distressing enough for a high wall to be constructed at the end of the castle gardens in the nineteenth century, ostensibly to protect Queen Victoria from being subjected to such offensive sights. Aloft one of the surviving towers within the castle confines stands a statue of Justice which has long been the subject of Dublin humour; built with her back to the city, she is forever mocked as representing precisely the kind of justice Dubliners should expect from the British.

On the original Viking settlement of Dublin west of the Castle stand two Church of Ireland Cathedrals within a stone's throw of each other. Christ Church was Dublin's earliest Cathedral and was originally built of wood in 1038 by the first Christian king of the Norsemen. Demolished and rebuilt in stone by Strongbow in 1172, it thus became a monument to the first English incursion into Ireland, whilst the Archbishop at Strongbow's time, Lorcan or Laurence O'Toole became Dublin's patron saint. St Patrick's Cathedral is the largest church in Ireland and was built over the well St Patrick used for baptism in the fifth century. The cathedral has had a chequered career structurally, being not only repeatedly damaged by tempest, fire and not quite flood - it has no crypt as what remains of the River Poddle flows beneath it - but in the seventeenth century having suffered the indignity of being used as stabling for Cromwell's horses. Two centuries earlier, the Earls of Ormonde and Kildare were apparently arguing furiously in the Cathedral until Kildare finally offered a reconciliatory hand to his foe through a hole he hacked in the door between them. The quarrel was resolved, the arm remained intact, and the incomplete door can still be seen at the west end of the Cathedral, giving rise, legend has it, to the expression, "chancing one's arm." Jonathon Swift, the acerbic satirist and author, was Dean of St Patrick's between 1713 and his death in 1745, and in his crusade against inequality in Ireland suggested memorably that the Irish burn everything English except their coal. He is buried in the Cathedral where the powerful and bitter Latin epitaph he wrote himself reads, "He is laid where furious indignation can no longer lacerate his heart."

Since Ireland attained constitutional independence and her own Parliament in 1921, the lower and upper houses, the Dail and Seanad respectively, have met at the austere and dignified Leinster House on Kildare Street. Built by Richard Castle, who was responsible for many of Ireland's loveliest buildings, Leinster House was commissioned by the Earl of Kildare in 1745, and began life as Kildare House until the Earl assumed the title Duke of Leinster.

The Long Room, Trinity College

Kildare was much ribbed for building a house south of the Liffey when smart society was based to the north, however his prediction that, "where I go, society will follow" proved right and Leinster House now stands at the hub of the city. Given the position of the house, it is perhaps less surprising that it has two entirely different faces; from the town and Kildare Street it appears to be a classical town house, whilst from Merrion Square and what was at the time countryside, it has the appearance of a fine country residence.

Fitzwilliam Square, Merrion Square and the immediate surroundings lie at the heart of what remains of Georgian Dublin. The elegant squares and graceful entrances flanked by pillars, surmounted by peacock fanlights and ornamented only by brightly polished knockers are a wonderful testament to the easy confidence of Georgian formal planning. The Georgians were consummate designers and architects and their flair for creating perfect simplicity and proportion transformed any potential for uniformity into the gracious beauty so typical of Dublin's Georgian heritage. Merrion Square East, which ran into Fitzwilliam Street Lower,

The Bank of Ireland *College Green*

was in fact the longest unbroken line of Georgian houses in Europe until 26 of them fell victim to an architectural tragedy of twentieth century planning and were obliterated to make way for an office block.

North of the Liffey, O'Connell Street is the city's main thoroughfare and probably Dublin's most famous, or infamous, street due to the events of the Easter Rising. It also has the distinction of having been frequently rechristened in a strange chronology of Dublin's history. In the early eighteenth century it was called Drogheda Street after Viscount Henry Moore, Earl of Drogheda, who in his vanity contrived to have as many streets thereabouts named after him as possible, even to the inclusion of "Of Lane". By the middle of the century, it had been widened to a stately 45 metres by Luke Gardiner, later Viscount Mountjoy, who was responsible for much of the early development of Dublin north of the Liffey, and who gave it the name of Gardiner's Mall. After a period as Sackville Street, it finally became known as O'Connell Street in 1924, after Daniel O'Connell, the Irish nationalist leader and patriot whose greatest achievement was to secure emancipation for the Catholics in the early nineteenth century. It has long been a subject of wry humour that one of the principal streets in the capital of such a deeply moral Catholic nation should once have been graced by statues commemorating O'Connell, Parnell and Nelson, all three of them acknowledged adulterers, although Nelson's statue was felled by an IRA attack in 1966.

To the west of O'Connell Street lies the aptly named Rotunda Hospital, the first maternity hospital in either Ireland or Britain, which was built in 1757 using the plans of Leinster House as an economy measure. Just opposite the hospital, the conveniently located Patrick Conway pub, which dates from 1745 has, no doubt, been offering not only moral support, but copious quantities of Guinness, Ireland's "black gold", to expectant fathers ever since the hospital first opened its doors.

Guinness is an earthly pleasure with almost mystical resonance for the Irish. Situated at St James's Gate in the Liberties, an area so called as it lay beyond the jurisdiction of mediaeval Dublin, the Guinness Brewery was founded in 1759 by Arthur Guinness, who, with £100 in his pocket, set up not only a national institution but what is now the largest brewery in Europe. More than half the beer consumed in Ireland comes from St James's Gate, and of the 900 million pints brewed every year, 300 million are exported annually.

There are hundreds of splendid watering holes in Dublin, but perhaps the pub with the most famous literary connotations is Davy Byrne's, where Leopold Bloom, of Ulysses fame, ate gorgonzola and mustard sandwiches washed down with Burgundy for lunch. Every year fans of the Dublin born James Joyce follow Bloom's peregrinations around Dublin on "Bloomsday", June 16th, on a pilgrimage which includes not only a pause for the obligatory sandwich but also a visit to Sweny, the old chemist in Lincoln place, to buy, as did Bloom in 1904, a bar of lemon soap.

The South East

The counties of Kildare, Wicklow, Wexford, Waterford, Kilkenny, and Carlow are predominantly a region of rich farmland and golden beaches; the driest and sunniest corner of Ireland where the granite Wicklow Mountains dominate the horizons and the ancient legacy of the Vikings still suffuses the major towns of the region.

To the west of Dublin, Kildare is a county of bogland and rolling plain, where the famous Bog of Allen in the north transforms the rich southern pastures which nurture Ireland's precious bloodstock industry into a desolate brown wasteland. Although close to Dublin and thus at the heart of the English Pale, Kildare, and indeed much of Ireland, was controlled between the twelfth and sixteenth centuries by the all-powerful Anglo-Norman Fitzgerald family, Earls of Kildare. What equilibrium existed then was shattered when Silken Thomas Fitzgerald, so called for the tassles on his followers' helmets, rebelled unsuccessfully against the English crown in 1536, prompting Henry VIII to take an unwelcome interest in Ireland that led directly to the centuries of conflict which have tainted Irish history.

That Kildare was in the traditionally safe territory of the Pale did, however, give the wealthy Ascendancy a confidence that resulted in their building some of the most magnificent stately homes in Ireland. The Fitzgeralds, who after various setbacks regained their wealth and position, commissioned the ubiquitous and talented Richard Castle to build Carton House in the mid eighteenth century in Maynooth. Exquisite as it was, Carton paled into insignificance when compared with the extravagant splendour of Castletown House in nearby Celbridge. An immense Palladian mansion designed by Alessandro Galilei, Castletown was built for William "Speaker" Conolly, whose humble origins did not preclude his amassing an enormous fortune that not only made him the richest man in Ireland, but gave him the wherewithal to build the largest private house in the country. Castletown's flamboyant and magnificent stuccowork was a product of the inspired and brilliant Francini brothers, whose timely appearance in Ireland and subsequent contribution to the splendid interiors of so many Ascendancy houses was a happy coincidence brought about by their being shipwrecked off Ireland en route to America.

In the north of Kildare the enormous and ancient Bog of Allen is the best example of a raised peat bog in Ireland and once covered a staggering 100,000 hectares. Peat was one of the major sources of fuel in Ireland and bogs have long been worked not only for this, but also more recently for gardening purposes; as a result the boglands which featured so often in Irish mythology are fast disappearing, to the extent that they are now the target of environmental conservationists.

Ardmore

Peat bog

It is, however, as the mecca of the Irish horse racing world that Kildare is best known. The multi-million pound bloodstock industry centres around the plain of Curragh, a huge limestone plateau which reputedly produces unbeatable pasture for forming strong bones. The world famous Kildare studs harness this natural phenomenon with a highly skilled breeding programme to produce racehorses sporting price tags that defy the imagination. Earlier this century Colonel Hall founded what is now the National Stud and later donated it to the British Crown, for which generosity he was elevated to Lord Wavertree. His indisputably successful, if unconventional, methods relied heavily on a bizarre belief in horoscopes which entailed, amongst other things, orienting the stabling for his horses to reap the full benefits of the all important astral aspects. Within the vicinity Curragh, Punchestown and Naas are three of Ireland's most famous race tracks, where people from all walks of life come to enjoy what has become one of Ireland's favourite national pastimes, as well as one of the country's major sources of income.

South of Dublin, Wicklow's landscapes include some of the best and wildest of Irish scenery. The desolate brown and purple Wicklow Mountains and deep dark glens traditionally provided ideal cover for bandits in the eighteenth century and by the 1798 Rebellion Wicklow had become such a hotbed of Gaelic resistance that the British were forced to cut a route through the mountains to the south of the county in an attempt to control the rebels. The Military Road still exists and given the mountainous and boggy terrain it crossed, must have posed quite some test of early nineteenth century engineering skills.

As in Kildare, the influence of nearby Dublin produced an array of great houses built by the Ascendancy, including Powerscourt, a fabulous mid eighteenth century mansion designed by Richard Castle which was tragically destroyed by fire just as renovations had been completed in 1974. The picturesque village of Enniskerry was planned to complement the house, which is famed for not only the idyllic setting overlooking the Wicklow mountains, but also for its magnificent formal gardens. The Italian garden reputedly took 100 men twelve years to complete whilst near the estate boundary Powerscourt Waterfall, the highest in Britain or Ireland, tumbles ninety dramatic metres to the ground below. Richard Castle also designed the enormous Palladian Russborough House, whose elegant silver grey granite frontage stretches for an extraordinary 275 metres and is, not surprisingly, the longest in Ireland. Russborough became the template for many Georgian houses in Ireland and, as was often the case, was spectacularly adorned inside with plasterwork by the Francini brothers.

Just south of Russborough lies the magical valley of Glendalough, or glen of the two lakes. High in the hills, Glendalough is one of the most spellbinding enclaves of Christianity in Ireland. Ancient monastic ruins are scattered throughout the valley, enhancing the landscape to create an atmosphere of spirituality and stillness that is eerily compelling. Saint Kevin, of the royal house of Leinster, founded a monastery in the valley in the sixth century, having abandoned a previous ambition to become a hermit after his reputation for saintliness infallibly attracted hordes of followers. In the absence of towns prior to the advent of the Vikings, monastic settlements formed the centres of population in Ireland and Glendalough rapidly became a major contributor to the country's reputation as the Land of Saints and Scholars, surviving the vicissitudes of early Irish history until it finally collapsed as a monastic community in the seventeenth century.

South of Wicklow the south eastern corner of Ireland is taken up by the county of Wexford, where glorious sandy beaches and low gentle hills were the backdrop to the initial Anglo-Norman invasion of Ireland in the latter half of the twelfth century. The town of Wexford was settled by the Vikings in 850 AD at the mouth of a river, as was the Viking norm, whence it acquired the name Waesfjord, meaning sandy harbour. The narrow streets of the town are an atmospheric reminder of its ancient roots whilst the site of what was the mediaeval Bull Ring bore witness to the unspeakable actions of Cromwell who, in his crusade to crush the Catholics and obliterate the Jacobites, put 1500 of the 2000 men, women and children of Wexford to death in 1649 after the town refused to surrender.

Western Wexford is bounded by the isolation of the Hook Peninsula, which featured famously in Cromwell's professed determination to take Waterford town by Hook or by Crooke, the latter referring to the tiny village which lies next to Waterford harbour. Between the peninsula and Bannow Bay, where the Anglo-Normans, or in fact Strongbow's Welsh contingent, first arrived in 1169, the lovely ruins of Tintern Abbey greatly improve what is otherwise a less than captivating setting. The strange choice of location arose from a promise that William

Marshall, Strongbow's son-in-law, made whilst caught in a violent tempest offshore to the effect that should he survive, he would build an abbey wherever his boat brought him to land. Further down the peninsula Baginbun Head was another focus of the initial Anglo-Norman landings, where the mighty ramparts the invaders constructed to make a beachhead whilst awaiting reinforcements are still just visible. As the rocky and lonely shore sweeps down towards the west, what is probably the world's oldest lighthouse crowns the extremity of Hook Head. Legend has it that monks lit a beacon on the headland in the fifth century, eliciting such gratitude from the Vikings that with uncharacteristic generosity they left the holy brethen in peace. Raymond de Gros, one of the earliest Anglo-Normans to arrive in Ireland, later constructed a lighthouse at the end of the twelfth century, the remains of which have been incorporated into the tower that still warns shipping of the dangers to hand.

The Hook Peninsula forms the eastern flank of Waterford Harbour, a superb deep natural harbour far inland on the River Suir that presented an irresistibly appealing prospect to the Vikings. Waterford thrived on the basis of its waterborne trade and at the end of the twelfth century Henry II declared it a royal city in the hope of securing the allegiance of the townspeople to the English Crown. At the end of the eighteenth century, the Waterford Crystal factory was established in the town, producing exquisite hand blown and hand cut glass of exceptional quality. The factory survived until 1851, when it was forced to close due to the heinous commercial restrictions imposed by the British hegemony on Irish trade. The factory was reopened in 1947, since when beautiful heavy lead crystal creations have been produced by a team of cutters and blowers who painstakingly learn their delicate trade over a period of five years.

Throughout Ireland's landscapes the horizon is occasionally pierced by elegant tapering round towers, the finest and most spectacular of which is a twelfth century tower which soars thirty metres into the sky at Ardmore, where Saint Declan founded a monastery several decades before Saint Patrick had even arrived in Ireland. In the terrifying times of Viking invasion the monasteries of Ireland suffered appallingly time and time again, hence tall round towers became a prominent feature of early monasteries as lookouts and refuges. The entrances were far enough above ground level to be cut off once the brethren had climbed to safety and although the Irish name, cloigtheach, means house of the bell, round towers were not built primarily as campaniles. Considering the remarkable height, strength and stability of these graceful ancient towers, it is abundantly clear that the skills of the early masons were consummate; their legacy has become one of Ireland's most characteristic architectural glories.

Of an entirely different architectural genre, Lismore Castle is a pale grey castellated flight of fantasy, built originally in 1185 but embellished to its present majestic form in the mid nineteenth century by the English architect Paxton. Overlooking the lovely valley of the River Blackwater, Lismore was given to Sir Walter Raleigh in the sixteenth century, who then

View of Kilkenny
William Ashford
(1746 - 1824)

sold it to Richard Boyle, Earl of Cork. It was his son, Robert, who was born in the castle who established the relationship between gaseous temperature, volume and pressure, earning a reputation in the process as the father of modern chemistry rather than the esoteric art of alchemy. Lismore eventually passed to the Dukes of Devonshire in the mid eighteenth century, under whose patronage Paxton's experimental use of glass and iron culminated in the construction of Crystal Palace in London in 1851.

Inland from Waterford, Kilkenny is a charming pastoral county and was once part of the Kingdom of Ossory which existed until the twelfth century. Inevitably, given its attractions, Kilkenny was settled by the Vikings and after 1171 the county's history became irrevocably enmeshed with that of the mighty Butler family, Earls of Ormond. The Butlers, who had adopted their name after being appointed Chief Butlers of Ireland by Henry II, derived an enormous income from the butlerage, or duty, on wine imported into either England or Ireland, which explained the three glasses of wine on the family shield and also generated a princely sum in 1811 when one of the family, finding himself a bit short of cash, sold the rights for £216,000.

The city of Kilkenny is one of the most attractive mediaeval cities in Ireland, its origins reaching back as far as the first century BC when it was the capital of the Kingdom of Ossory, ruled by Aengus Ossraigh. Named for the monastery of Saint Canice, Cill Chainnigh or Kilkenny was controlled by the Ossraigh, later Fitzpatrick, family until the Anglo-Normans arrived in the twelfth century. Under their influence the city flourished to the extent that it eventually became the unofficial capital of Ireland and home to the Kilkenny parliament which passed the infamous 1366 Statutes of Kilkenny, a crude attempt by the English to halt the process of Anglo-Norman integration into native Irish society.

South of the city, Jerpoint Abbey is one of the most impressive ruined Cistercian monasteries in Ireland. Established in the early twelfth century by one of the Kings of Ossory, Jerpoint was beautifully embellished during the fourteenth and fifteenth centuries to become worlds apart from the simple austerity and architectural understatement that characterised the early Cistercian foundations. Legend has it that Santa Claus, or Saint Nicholas, was buried near the Abbey after the Knights of Jerpoint brought his body back with them on their return from the Crusades.

Tucked alongside the east of Kilkenny, Carlow is the second smallest county in Ireland and despite its diminutive size and proximity to Dublin proved a constant thorn in the flesh to the English during the Middle Ages. That the town of Carlow lay on the border of the Pale was of no significance to the defiantly patriotic Gaels, whose hostile attitude forced the English to bribe their officials based in the castle to risk the not inconsiderable perils of Carlow life. The Kings of Leinster, the MacMurrough Kavenaghs, were particularly adept at beating the English at their own game in the fourteenth century and even at the end of the eighteenth century a fierce nucleus of Gaelic resistance remained in the county, leading to the death of over 600 rebels in the 1798 Rising.

Carlow's other claim to fame lies at Browne's Hill, where one of Europe's largest dolmens glowers over the local landscape. The huge 5000 year old capstone weighs more than 100 tonnes, and proved an insurmountable problem even to those experts in stone architecture; one end of it rests on the ground, whilst the other is supported in the normal way on sturdy boulders. Derived from the Breton word for stone table, dolmens were the tombs in which bodies were laid and legend relates that every dolmen in Ireland sheltered Diarmuid and Grainne for a night during the epic saga of their flight from the jilted Finn MacCool, leader of the fabled Fianna warriors. Grainne was King Cormac's goddess daughter and Diarmuid one of the King's warriors; they eloped on the eve of her wedding to Finn MacCool, who pursued them untiringly for a year in his determination to recover his beloved betrothed.

Kilkenny Castle

Cork and Kerry

The beautiful counties of Cork and Kerry lie at the south western extremity of Ireland, their spectacular coastlines buffeted by the Atlantic waves and weather, but spared extremes of temperature by the benign influence of the Gulf Stream. Some of the loveliest landscapes of Ireland are to be found here, the mesmerising tranquillity of Cork's lush countryside contrasting startlingly with the splendour of neighbouring Kerry's wilder and more rugged beauty.

The city of Cork is Ireland's second largest city and a friendly rival to Dublin. It is an intimate place; relaxed but vibrant, intensely Irish and yet flaunting a colourful and surprisingly cosmopolitan air. The city dates from the seventh century when St Finbarr founded an abbey and school by the River Lee, whence the Gaelic name Corcaigh, meaning marshy ground, arose. During the seventeenth and eighteenth centuries it became Europe's premier port for dairy products, particularly butter, which was produced locally and salted for export worldwide. Surrounding the centre of Cork, which lies on an island midstream, the multitude of quays which generated its considerable mercantile wealth still line the shores of the river, whilst on the island Grand Parade is but one of several streets which display their origins as waterways with moorings still anchored to the pavement.

During the mid nineteenth century Cork became one of the main points of departure for the flood of starving victims escaping the Great Famine, who contributed greatly to the staggering statistic that since 1820, more than half the people born in Ireland have emigrated. In the latter half of the century Cork became an important centre for the Fenian movement, creating an intellectual base for the nationalist struggle in which Cork later became a focal point. It was here that the Black and Tans waged a particularly vicious war against the Republicans in which much of the city was burnt, and nearby that Michael Collins, commander-in-chief of the IRA, was shot during the Civil War that followed the Anglo-Irish Treaty of 1921.

In Shandon, on the north bank of the River Lee, St Anne's Church is renowned not only for the evocative peal of its bells but the fact that the pretty bell tower is surmounted by the extraordinary sight of a large salmon, broadcasting the unpopular fact that the monks had apparently decided to keep salmon fishing rights on the river to themselves. St Finbarr's Cathedral on the opposite bank could not be more different. Nineteenth century Gothic church architecture is one of Cork's constant features and the cathedral is a spectacular confection in the French style of the thirteenth century, its slender spire soaring gracefully upwards to dominate the south Cork skyline.

Cobh Harbour *last sight of Ireland for countless emigrants*

Blarney Castle

Just outside the city, the Blarney stone high up in Blarney Castle is one of Ireland's enduring legends; the story goes that Lord Blarney, having promised to surrender his castle to the English, so exasperated Queen Elizabeth I and her deputies with his perpetual prevarication and avoidance of any kind of action, that she was provoked into exploding, "Blarney, Blarney, what he says he does not mean, it is the usual Blarney". And so the term was coined and with it the tradition that kissing the stone, a far from easy feat, bestows upon the kisser untold powers of persuasion and cajolery - the "gift of the gab" as it is less than romantically called in the vernacular.

Cork's coast is rich with maritime history; the safe natural harbour of Cobh was the city of Cork's original port and became known as Queenstown during the nineteenth century after Queen Victoria landed there in 1849. The first transatlantic steamship left from Cobh in 1838 and it was also the last port of call the doomed Titanic was to make before setting off on her first and only crossing to America. Further down the coast, Youghal lies at the mouth of the Blackwater, one of Ireland's best salmon rivers, and was reputedly where Sir Walter

Raleigh planted the first potato on his return from the New World. The ramifications of such an apparently trivial action on the fate of Ireland, he could, no doubt, have barely imagined. Raleigh had been granted Youghal and 40,000 surrounding acres by Elizabeth I in the plantations, and although he was Mayor in 1588, took little interest in Ireland, preferring to spend his time writing poetry with his friend, Edmund Spenser, whose "Faerie Queen" so flattered Elizabeth that he too was granted estates nearby.

Youghal's mediaeval town walls are some of the best preserved in Ireland and survived Cromwell's infamous tour of destruction in 1649 when the incumbent English garrison diplomatically chose to side with him rather than the King. Thus the town remained intact and the thirteenth century water gate through which Cromwell left for the docks in his final departure from Ireland has ever since been known as Cromwell's Arch.

The picturesque port of Kinsale did not have such a lucky escape from potential disaster when in 1601 a Spanish fleet arrived to support the Irish against Elizabeth I's forces. Hugh O'Neill's army was in the north of the country and the town was besieged by the English until the weary men, who had marched the entire length of Ireland, arrived. Not surprisingly they were defeated and not only did this herald the death of Gaelic Ireland, but on a more local scale, Catholics were banned from the town for a hundred years. Meanwhile, Kinsale thrived as a shipbuilding centre and it was from here that Alexander Selkirk set off on a voyage which left him stranded on a desert island for years, inspiring Daniel Defoe with the plot for Robinson Crusoe.

Inland from Kinsale lies the Protestant town of Bandon, which was so virulently anti-Catholic in the seventeenth century that inscribed on the city walls were the words,

> *"Jew, Turk or atheist may enter here, but not a papist."*

The retort beneath ran along the lines,

> *"Whoever wrote this wrote it well, for the same is written on the gates of hell."*

Dispossessed and downtrodden the Catholics of the time may have been, lacking in humour they were certainly not.

At the western end of Cork, three spectacular peninsulae reach into the Atlantic ocean. Mizen Head and Sheep's Head are similar in that they epitomise the Ireland of verdant and idyllic landscapes, whilst Breara Peninsula is harsh and rocky, the scenery wilder and the views more starkly beautiful. Between Sheep's Head and Breara lies Bantry Bay, the scene of a near miss which could have drastically altered the entire course of Irish history. In 1796 a French fleet supporting the United Irishmen against the English arrived in Bantry Bay in such ferociously violent storms that of the original 43 ships, only 16 reached Ireland and of those, none managed to land. Bantry House, which overlooks the bay with one of the most stupendous views in the country, was the home of Richard White, who alerted the Cork militia to the presence of the fleet, and was elevated to a peerage for his troubles. Built in 1771, it was a carefree amalgam of architectural styles and typified the exuberance of the Protestant Ascendancy whose love of the good life and fine things was manifested in so many beautiful houses of eighteenth century Ireland.

In a sublime position set against the stunning backdrop of the mountains of the peninsula stand the ruins of Dunboy Castle, stronghold of the O'Sullivans who ruled the area for three hundred years before the English arrived in 1602. Copper was discovered locally in 1810 and mined by the men, women and children of the area, generating an enormous fortune for the Puxley family, whose spooky but magnificent Gothic mansion lies in ruins after the IRA burnt it down in 1922. The Puxleys were the subject of Hungry Hill, Daphne du Maurier's novel, which took its title from the highest point on the peninsula, whence the views are breathtaking and the panorama sweeps dramatically in all directions.

Kerry is a wild and romantic county, where mountains meet the sea in splendid juxtaposition and heather clad moorland gives way to silver loughs set into the landscape like precious stones. The mystical atmosphere of Kerry is greatly heightened by the ancient sites and monuments which abound throughout the county whilst the slanting light which comes in off the sea suffuses the entire landscape with an aura that is almost surreal.

Centuries ago Ireland was densely forested, largely by sessile oaks, which are characterised by their short trunks and strangely hunched form. One of the few remaining examples of these primeval oaks is found near Kenmare, in the Uragh Woods, whilst from Kenmare itself the views over Macgillycuddy's Reeks are spectacular; what the mountains lack in stature is entirely overshadowed by a grandeur that belies their relatively small size.

Beyond the Gap of Dunloe, a wild gorge separating Macgillycuddy's Reeks from the Purple Mountain, so called for the heather which swathes its slopes, lies the beautiful Lough Learne and the ruin of Ross Castle. Ross, from the Gaelic for peninsula, stands on the shores of the lough and was the last bastion of resistance to Cromwell's forces in the area. Legend had it that the castle would only fall to attack from the water and when the wily General Ludlow, commander of the English, learnt of this he put his troops in boats to approach the castle from the lough. The battle hardened warriors in the castle, deeply dispirited at seeing the fulfilment of the prophecy, surrendered forthwith and thus the castle fell into English hands.

From Killarney, the justifiably famous Ring of Kerry follows the coast around the lovely Iveragh Peninsula, where the combination of mountainous landscapes sweeping down to endless seascapes, soft air and seductive evening light make for an ever changing view that ranges from the spellbinding to the exhilarating.

At the end of the peninsula, the shores surrounding Derrynane House once nurtured an active smuggling trade, whence derived much of the wealth of the landowning Catholic

Gallarus Oratory

O'Connell family. The O'Connells managed to evade the Penal Laws restricting land ownership and in 1825 the house passed to Daniel O'Connell, the peaceable campaigner whose greatest achievement was emancipation for the Catholics and whose inherited wealth made it possible for him to pursue a career in politics. The dining room in the house is resplendent with furniture and silver from grateful Catholics, perhaps the most outstanding gift being the dining room table which took two men four years to carve and embellish.

Off the neighbouring headland, the rocky crags of Great Skellig, or Skellig Michael, and Little Skellig rear abruptly from the sea in lonely isolation. Battered by the full force of the ocean, anywhere less hospitable is hard to imagine, yet the monks of the early Irish monastic movement found solace and fulfilment in the austerity of life in such remote locations. They were influenced by the Egyptian Coptic Church founded in the deserts of Egypt and Lybia, and sought the ultimate test of faith by living the simplest and most ascetic of lives. Between the seventh and thirteenth centuries, the monks of Skellig Michael battled across the sea to live in tiny dry stone beehive huts perched 500 vertigo-inducing feet above the crashing waves of the Atlantic. The name derives from skeilig, Gaelic for splinter of stone, Skellig Michael being dedicated to Saint Michael, guardian against the powers of darkness and patron of high places, after he helped St Patrick drive the last of the serpents in Ireland from the island.

Every August, the small town of Killorglin on the Iveragh Peninsula honours the wild goat with "Puck's Fair", a three day event commemorating the narrow escape the town had from Cromwell's forces after a herd of wild goats chased through the streets heralding the arrival of his troops. A wild goat is "enthroned" as King Puck in the town square, and thereafter the town explodes into a riotous celebration of bacchanalian proportions. The fair's origins are, however, much earlier than Cromwell's era; the pagan Celtic festival of Lughnasa was a three day feast, which celebrated the start of the harvest with, amongst other heathen rites, ritual sacrifices.

To the north the magnificent landscapes of the Dingle Peninsula are dotted with a multitude of ring forts, high crosses, early Christian monuments and Celtic relics. The town of Dingle lies near the end of the peninsula and is remarkable for the fact that it was virtually the only place in Ireland where an attempt to convert the local Catholics to Protestantism was anything but a dismal failure. Curate Goodman elected the non-confrontational route and chose to persuade his potential flock by preaching to them in Gaelic and building schools and houses for his converts. It was an admirable mixture of bribery and cajolery which had a greater success rate than any of the less tactful methods employed elsewhere.

West of Dingle the people of the peninsula remain Gaelic speaking, and it is here that a staggering concentration of ancient monuments is to be found. Of these the Gallarus Oratory is probably the most outstanding, and beautifully illustrates the extraordinary skill of the early masons who built it. As in the beehive huts found on Skellig Michael, the dry stone technique was an immensely successful method of construction and although the Oratory dates from between the ninth and twelfth century, it is still in almost perfect condition. The masonry remains weatherproof and the only sign of ageing is a slight sag amidships of the upturned boat shaped roof.

Close by, Kilmalkedar Church was built on an earlier pagan site from which a fine ogham stone and a rare alphabet stone remain. The written form of Celtic between the fourth and seventh centuries, ogham script was named after the Celtic god of writing, Ogmios, whilst the alphabet stone was the equivalent of an ogham latin dictionary, on which latin and ogham characters were inscribed side by side. From the church the Saint's Road, dedicated to St Brendan, scales the peak of Mount Brandon, Ireland's second highest mountain. It was from the summit of this beautiful and often mist shrouded mountain that St Brendan the Navigator saw a vision of the Blessed Land and resolved to set out in search of it. With twelve monks, he sailed to the Orkneys, Wales, Iceland and what may have been the east coast of America in a leather and wooden boat, the story of which epic voyage was committed to paper six hundred years later in the eleventh century Navigato Brendan.

The Gap of Dunloe *Ring of Kerry*

Limerick, Tipperary, and Clare

Bordered by the great River Shannon to the north and a scattering of mountains to the south, Limerick is a county of fertile lands and historic castles, the former an irresistible magnet which attracted first the Vikings and then the great Anglo-Norman families, the latter a legacy of those mediaeval invaders and settlers. Of the Anglo-Normans, it was the great dynasty of the Fitzgeralds, Earls of Desmond, which held sway in the surrounding area, becoming so Gaelicized over the years and accruing such power that the measures taken by their Tudor overlords to bring them into line resulted in a major uprising during 1571. Limerick, and much of the province of Munster, was plunged into a savage conflict which eventually brought about the ruin of the Geraldines, as the family and their supporters were known, whilst also beginning a notable history of local resistance to English dominion.

The city of Limerick was founded by the Vikings at the most westerly fording point of the Shannon in the tenth century. Despite an otherwise somewhat lacklustre setting, (the Gaelic name means barren spot of land), Limerick was fought over, burnt to the ground, destroyed and decimated on so many occasions during the following two centuries that the city motto, "an ancient city well studied in the arts of war" smacks not only of Irish humour, but also of extreme understatement. With the Anglo-Normans came relative calm and also the city walls, which in 1650 held Cromwell at bay in a siege lasting a year, and which forty years later separated William of Orange's troops from the last bastion of Jacobite resistance in Ireland. In 1691 the Irish Jacobite commander, Patrick Sarsfield, was finally forced to surrender to the Williamite forces and sign the Treaty of Limerick, which signalled both the triumph of Protestant over Catholic and the start of an era of abject misery for the native Irish.

The castle of Limerick which finally fell to the Williamites was King John's Castle; new military technology in the form of cannons demanded far stronger defences than had been required before and thus the thirteenth century castle became one of the most formidable English strongholds in the country and remains an exceptional example of Anglo-Norman fortification. The castle guarded Thomond Bridge, across which is the stone where the Treaty was signed in 1691 - the Stone of the Violated Treaty it is called locally.

South of Limerick is the lovely horseshoe shaped Lough Gur where the aura of mystery which emanates from the surrounding ancient sites is left wonderfully intact by a lack of modern intrusion upon the landscape. One of the most impressive stone circles in Ireland lies nearby, its almost perfect 4000 year old symmetry described by 113 huge stones, whilst scattered on the hillsides are standing stones, burial mounds and various other prehistoric remains which bear testament to a civilisation whose physical legacy has imbued much of Ireland with a compelling and powerful sense of antiquity.

Lough Gur *celtic cross*

In the centre of Lough Gur, the rise of land called Knockadoon was once surrounded by water and connected to the shore only by a drawbridge from Bouchier's Castle, a typical fifteenth century Desmond tower castle. Of the staggering 427 tower houses which once stood in Limerick, most of the ruins which indicate any significance were power bases of the Desmond family. Black Castle, which also stands sentinel to Knockadoon, predated tower house architecture and was the principal seat of the Desmonds between the fourteenth and seventeenth centuries whilst Castle Matrix, another fifteenth century Desmond tower house, has been spectacularly restored to its original glory, even to the painstaking recalculation of the admirably precise measurements required to build functional defensive rather than ornamental battlements.

Above the broad reaches of the Shannon and bordered by Galway Bay to the north and Lough Derg to the east, Clare is a spectacular county, where the land is mostly poor and the great limestone rockscapes of the Burren in the north possess a strange and desolate beauty. Until the fourth century, Clare was part of Connacht, the barrenness and infertility of which was forever recorded in Cromwell's displacement of the Irish in the mid seventeenth century from richer lands to "hell or Connacht". Thereafter, Connacht became the Kingdom of Thomond, ruled by the O'Briens, who were responsible for keeping Clare beyond the mainstream of Anglo-Norman influence by defeating the Norman de Clare family at Dysert O'Dea in 1318 and evicting them from the area. With the arrival of Henry VIII on the Irish scene in the sixteenth century, the O'Briens were brought onto the English side as Earls of Thomond, where they remained reasonably loyal to the crown until Cromwell's vicious campaign to crush the Gaelic Irish and the Royalists terrorised the country.

Ennis Friary

Clare has a proud place in Irish Republican history as one of the great bastions of nationalism; in 1828 Daniel O'Connell was elected MP for Clare with such a huge majority that the British Government was forced to lift the ban on Catholics sitting in Parliament and finally acquiesced to Catholic emancipation. Later that century, it was from Ennis, county town of Clare, that Charles Parnell first advocated the tactic of boycotting in the Land War and for East Clare that Eamon de Valera was TD (equivalent of MP) between 1917 and 1959, during which time he played a pre-eminent role in Irish politics and the Republic of Ireland came into existence.

Quin Abbey

At the beginning of the thirteenth century the Franciscans came to Ireland and unlike the Cistercians, who remained aloof from the Irish, became a popular order which identified with the instincts of the people and fulfilled their spiritual needs on a kindly and human scale. The Franciscan Friary in the centre of Ennis was built by the O'Brien Kings of Thomond in 1242 and evolved into one of the greatest seats of learning and education in Ireland during the fifteenth century. At the same time, the graceful and beautifully preserved Quin Abbey was founded by the MacNamaras and built, no doubt with a defiant element of humour, within the shell of a thirteenth century de Clare castle. Elegant belfry and lovely cloisters aside, Quin was also where the renowned duellist and splendidly named Fireballs MacNamara was buried. The MacNamaras were part of the O'Brien clan and controlled much of Clare until the middle of the fifteenth century. Of the phenomenal 42 castles they built in Clare, the finest are Bunratty, a faultlessly restored example of fifteenth century tower house architecture and Knappogue, which escaped the fate of so many Irish strongholds when Cromwell used it as his headquarters in 1649. After the Restoration of the Catholic monarchy in England, the MacNamaras regained ownership of their property, as did a few other lucky Irish families before Protestantism prevailed again under the auspices of William of Orange.

West of Knappogue lie the remains of the Moohaun Fort, one of Europe's largest Iron Age Hill forts which encloses nearly 13 hectares within three concentric ramparts. It was near here that in 1854 some railway workers unearthed one of Ireland's greatest hoards of prehistoric gold. The Great Clare Find, as it became known, yielded some stunning gold artefacts and the subsequent discovery of an exquisite gold necklace near Glenisheen in the north of Clare illustrated beautifully the talent of Ireland's prehistoric metal workers whose skills were legion and famed throughout Europe.

The westernmost point of Clare is Loop Head, a wind blasted headland thrusting into the Atlantic Ocean, where the views are inspiring and the legends enthralling. Loop Head is a corruption of Leap Head, and Irish mythology has it that Cuchulainn leapt from the headland to a stack far out to sea, and back again to escape the unwelcome attentions of the hag witch, Mal. He jumped successfully but Mal, who had pursued him mercilessly, fell and drowned, colouring the sea red with her blood and washing ashore on Hag's Head, to the north of which the west coast of Ireland comes to an abrupt and spectacular halt at the Cliffs of Moher. Stretching for five dramatic miles along the coast, the cliffs fall a sheer 230 metres into the thundering surf below.

Inland from the Cliffs of Moher the stark landscape of the Burren limestone plateau covers the north of Clare with a bare rocky countenance entirely at odds with the soft green Ireland of emerald isle fame. Despite the apparent desolation and infertility of the bleached and polished expanses, in spring the Burren bursts into a flamboyant display of colour with the many plants of arctic, alpine and Mediterranean origin which somehow flourish in the sparse soil and cracks in the limestone. The thin layer of topsoil which covered the Burren must also have provided enough of a foothold for the people who left more than 2500 ancient sites strewn across the rocks. Ancient unpaved highways, or green lanes, dating back thousands of years traverse the region whilst more recent castle ruins are scattered throughout. Beneath the plateau is an eerie labyrinth of caves, potholes and underground rivers into which drain the temporary lakes, or turloughs, which form on the Burren after heavy rain. Undersea caves, contorted rock formations, fantastic caverns and what is reputedly the tallest stalactite in western Europe are all accessible from Doolin, whose pubs also have the distinction of being great exponents of Clare's Irish folk music traditions.

To the east of Limerick and Clare, and quite different from them, Tipperary is one of the richest counties in Ireland, reaping its wealth from the luscious and fertile pastures of the Golden Vale. Although the centre of Tipperary is uncompromisingly flat, it is nonetheless very beautiful and the view from Slievenamon, the "mountain of the fairy women", over the scenic Galtee Mountains to the south and the dramatic Rock of Cashel to the north is idyllic.

Of all the remarkable sights in Ireland, there can be few as physically arresting and atmospherically moving as the Rock of Cashel. Set amid a vast grassy plain, the rock rises, apropos of nothing, 200 feet from the surrounding swards and is crowned with high stone walls surrounding an enclave of architectural treasures. Of these, which include a magnificent mediaeval cathedral, a unique High Cross and a Round Tower, the matchless early twelfth century Cormac Chapel is deemed by many to be Ireland's first major work of architecture. Cashel, from Caiseal meaning fortress, was once the ancient capital of the Kings of Munster, which title was held from the tenth century onwards by the O'Brien clan, who wrested the rock from their predecessors, the MacCarthys, under the leadership of Brian Boru. The royal

Cashel

seat of power was transformed into a religious stronghold when in 1101 one of the O'Brien kings gave the rock to the Church, soon after which Cormac MacCarthy commissioned what is now the most exquisite Romanesque chapel in Ireland.

Geology disagrees, but legend has it that the rock was formed when the Devil took a chunk out of the Slieve Bloom hills from "Devil's Bit", and dropped it whilst flying over the plain either because it tasted vile or because the sight of St Patrick preaching infuriated him so much that he spat it out in rage. It was here, also, that Ireland supposedly acquired the shamrock as the country's unofficial emblem, when St Patrick picked one nearby to explain the concept of the Trinity growing from one stem.

Tipperary's mediaeval history was dominated locally by the great Butler family, whose castles are still to be seen throughout the county. Of the many Butler strongholds in Tipperary, easily the most magnificent is the castle built on the River Suir at Cahir during the thirteenth and fifteenth centuries. At the time of building, it was Ireland's most imposing castle and even now its massive and virtually intact bulk conveys an awe inspiring impression of power. At the other extreme, in the sixteenth century, the tenth Earl of Ormonde, defied the norms of the day by doing the unheard of and building a completely unfortified English style mansion at Carrick-on-Suir as an extension to his existing fourteenth century castle. What must have been seen as madness in those turbulent times survived to become Ireland's finest, if not quite only, Elizabethan mansion, although the long awaited visit from Elizabeth I, in honour of which it was originally built, never apparently came to pass.

Galway, Mayo, and Roscommon

Galway is a county of contrasts, where the wild and elemental beauty of Connemara to the west is cleft from the flatter, more fertile east by Lough Corrib, the largest lough in the Republic. Galway is part of the province of Connacht, where the noble O'Conor dynasty reigned supreme for centuries by providing from their clan twenty four Kings of Connacht and eleven High Kings of Ireland. Although the Anglo-Normans did eventually gain a foothold in the city of Galway, the rest of the region remained resolutely Gaelic - no doubt the mountains, bogs and loughs which make it so compelling now presented a far from attractive proposition to the potential invaders who preferred to harvest the fat of Ireland from less challenging terrain. As a result Gaelic culture is still a way of life in Galway; more than half of the population speaks Gaelic, Connemara is Ireland's largest Gaeltacht, or Gaelic speaking area, there is a great tradition of Irish music and dancing in the many pubs and the 'crack' - the good times and the conversation - to be found in Galway city is as entertaining as any to be had in Ireland, especially during the famous Galway Race week and the International Oyster Fair.

Galway city was a small fishing village on the salmon filled waters of the River Corrib until the Anglo-Norman Richard de Burgo arrived and ousted the O'Flaherties from their castle in the town in the early thirteenth century. Although the name Galway possibly derived from gall, meaning foreigner, the de Burgo family rapidly succumbed to Gaelic influence and, changing their name to Burke, provoked Edward I into installing fourteen reliably loyal families to maintain control. Under these Anglo-Norman and Welsh merchants Galway grew into a prosperous trading centre, forging lucrative links with the Continent, whilst at the same time becoming a city state from which not only the Irish, but the Burkes were also excluded: 'no uninvited O' or Mac to show his face in Galway's fair streets' was the unequivocal edict. The furious and ferocious O'Flaherties, in conjunction with other local Irish clans, frequently attacked the town with a brutality that elicited the inscription, 'from the fury of the O'Flaherties, good Lord deliver us' on the city walls, but to no avail.

Galway and its merchant aristocracy remained intact and loyal to the crown until Cromwell and then William of Orange's forces inflicted grievous damage in the seventeenth century. Bar the physical damage, Cromwell's lasting legacy was the coining of the term City of Tribes, of whom the most powerful was the Lynch family. Their grip on the city was such that Lynches were mayors eighty times in less than two hundred years and it was from them that the expression lynch law derived when James Lynch condemned his son to death for killing a Spaniard and then had no choice but to carry out the sentence himself.

Lough Corrib

South of the fishing villages lining Galway Bay, where the oysters are second to none, an imposing and remarkably well preserved sixteenth century castle stands aloft a rocky outcrop commanding wonderful views over the coast. Dunguaire Castle was built on the site of a seventh century stronghold belonging to King Guaire, whose reputation for kindness and hospitality was such that his right arm was reputedly longer then his left from constantly giving away great quantities of gold. Doubtless the Fighting O'Flaherties were not afflicted with the same problem, although their sixteenth century tower castle fortress, Aughanure Castle, also stood on a rocky outcrop overlooking, in this case, the waters of Lough Corrib.

Surrounded by strikingly beautiful scenery, the 45 kilometre lough is a fisherman's dream, dotted with more than 360 islands, the largest and loveliest of which is Inchagoill. The name means devout stranger and on the island are several ancient remains including a burial stone bearing the oldest Latin legend in Ireland and possibly the oldest Christian inscription in the western world.

To the west of the lough, the dramatic and magnificent reaches of Connemara are dominated by the Twelve Bens and the quartzite Maumturk Mountains. Connemara is one of Ireland's loneliest and most spectacular regions, where the luminous western light can transform a bleak and eerie landscape into one of spectacular beauty and where the convoluted coast reveals crescent bays of sparkling white sand. Connemara's sparse population was laid waste

The Twelve Bens

and the town of Clifden, Connemara

during the famine, as was the case throughout the barren lands of Connacht; what attempts there were at eking an existence west of the lough were mostly on the islands off the coast, where monastic ruins testify to the hardiness of the monks of the holy orders.

One such monastery was founded by St Colman on the isle of Inishbofin after he fell out with the Church in England in 664 AD over the calculation of the date of Easter and removed himself to the tranquillity of island life in high dudgeon. The Gaelic name translates as isle of the white cow and legend has it that the island was permanently shrouded in mist until some fishermen inadvertently broke the spell by lighting a fire on the shore. As the mist cleared they saw a woman herding a white cow towards them, which turned to stone the moment she touched it with her stick. Under the apprehension that she was a witch, the fishermen attacked her whereupon, at their touch, she too was petrified into one of the two white rocks which lay on the shores of the lough until the nineteenth century. Cromwell used Inishbofin as a penal colony for priests during his reign of terror in Ireland, and in a particularly vicious display of nastiness chained one clergyman to Bishop's Rock to await his death with the incoming tide, in full view of his soldiers.

In the middle of Galway Bay lie the three Aran Islands whose isolation from the mainland has resulted in an all pervasive legacy of Gaelic culture. Gaelic remains the first language, full Gaelic dress was, until recently, fairly common and even now traditional waistcoats are frequently worn. The Aran sweaters which are a hallmark of the islands have, however, a melancholy aspect to their origins; they were knitted by the womenfolk of each family with different patterns to make identification of the drowned fishermen easier - presumably not an infrequent occurrence given the position of the islands fronting the full force of the Atlantic weather.

Dun Aengus

The pale sheets of rock that characterise the Aran Islands are a continuation of the limestone geology of the Burren, and whilst far from ideal, provided an environment infinitely preferable and easier to live in than the densely forested mainland of prehistoric Ireland. The remains of very early settlements are thus scattered over all three islands, the most extraordinary of which is without doubt Dun Aengus on the west coast of Inishmor. The fort's three semi-circular rings of dry stone masonry are almost impregnable in themselves without the added defence of a sheer plunge to the sea at the rear and an array of bristling and impassable chevaux de frise (jagged stones set at an angle into the ground) in front. In all it is an entirely menacing and professional arrangement, dating from possibly as far back as the Bronze Age, and theories are legion as to what terrifying aggressor warranted such defence in this remote outpost of Ireland. Perhaps the most bizarre is that the fort was built to withstand attack from the people of Atlantis to the west and that when the cataclysmic event that sunk Atlantis occurred, so the fort of Dun Aengus was riven in two and the missing half sent hurtling to the bottom of the ocean.

The Celtic heritage of Ireland is often given credit for the extraordinary artistic vision of the Irish and nowhere is this more exquisitely illustrated than in the Turoe Stone, discovered at an Iron Age fort near Loughrea. The stone is a granite boulder on which a sophisticated swirling design is carved in high relief. The delicacy of the workmanship is quite fantastic, especially given the obdurate nature of granite and reflects a direct influence from the La Tene culture in continental Europe which dates from around 300 BC; Celtic Ireland was obviously even then part of a larger European civilisation.

Lying above Galway, County Mayo's glorious coastline, desolate mountains and empty bogland endow it with a loveliness and an air of solitude that is immensely beguiling. Although the land is poor and Mayo has always been relatively unpopulated, the rivers and loughs provide some of the best fishing in Ireland and it is therefore little wonder that the ruins of Errew, Moyne, Rosserk, and in fact most of the abbeys in Mayo, are to be found where the canny monks could fish with ease. The twelfth century Augustinian abbey at Cong actually had a fishing hut on an island in the river, from which heavenly spot the monks would ring a bell every time a fish was caught.

Finlough, Delphi Lodge 1818-19
John Arthur O'Connor
(1792 - 1841)

The Marquis of Sligo, whose seat was at Westport in Mayo, was also a keen angler and christened his fishing lodge Delphi after travelling through Greece with Byron and seeing, in a flight of classical fantasy, similarities in the landscape, if presumably not the weather. The priceless treasures he brought back from his 'excavations' in Greece embellished Westport House, one of the finest Palladian mansions in Ireland which was built by Richard Castle in 1730 and whose opulent neo-classical interiors were designed by the Englishman, James Wyatt in the 1780s. The town of Westport is one of the prettiest examples of the planned towns of Ireland, in themselves unusual in the west of the country. The architects involved were again, as was so often the case with the Ascendancy and their Georgian legacy, Castle and Wyatt, whose vision of elegance and symmetry went as far as diverting the River Carrowbeg to flow down the centre of the Mall which runs through the town.

Westport lies near Clew Bay, territory of the feisty late sixteenth century pirate Grace O'Malley whose infamy derived as much from her marital history as her exploits at sea. Born of a seafaring family, she learnt the art of piracy at an early age, entirely eclipsing the first O'Flaherty husband with her contributions to his family coffers and soon becoming nominal head of the clan. After his death she was voted first woman chief of her own O'Malley clan and on choosing her next husband, a Burke, with a view to clinching total control over Clew Bay, resorted to Celtic right a year later and sacked him from one of his own castles, which she subsequently refused to relinquish. Grace had her own army and fleet and held such power at sea, and therefore over trade, that the desperate local merchants eventually pleaded with the English Governor to take the situation in hand; she was besieged in Rockfleet Castle, the almost perfect tower house where she divorced Burke, until she turned the tables on the English. Eventually pardoned by Elizabeth I, who reputedly held a grudging admiration for her, she was invited to court where she declined the offer of a title on the grounds that she was already a queen. Nonetheless, with an admirable eye to the future, she did accept the title of Viscount of Mayo for her son, and it is a direct descendent of hers who is the present Marquis of Sligo.

Overlooking Clew Bay, Croagh Patrick was the scene of momentous events of a different kind centuries beforehand. It was on this holy mountain, where the views are, in William Thackeray's words, 'the most beautiful in the world' that St Patrick retired for the forty days and nights of Lent, and where, with a flair for the dramatic which ranks him with the most consummate of performers, he summoned the 'venomous and loathsome creatures' of the country and banished them over the precipice of Lugnaharrib. To this day, there are no snakes in Ireland and every year tens of thousands of pilgrims make their way to the mountain summit on the last Sunday of July to venerate St Patrick and his miracles.

Inland from Galway and Mayo, Roscommon is an entirely landlocked county, although much of its border to the east is bounded by the River Shannon. The fishing in Roscommon is well renowned and despite the fact that most of the county is bog and grassland, the Curlew Mountains form a dramatic outline on the northern border.

Lying near the foot of one of the other rare mountains in Roscommon, Strokestown is a handsome planned town, in which the outstanding feature is the grandiose and surprisingly wide main street. Maurice Mahon, who was created Baron Hartland in 1800, had toured Vienna and having fallen under its magical spell determined to recreate a memory of the Ringstrasse in his home town. Whether this was the case, or whether he was an egotist who merely wanted to build the widest street in Europe is a moot point, but the avenue is certainly impressive and leads from the town to the imposing arched entrance of Strokestown Park House. The lands surrounding the house were originally granted to the Mahon family by Charles II in acknowledgement of their support for the Jacobite cause during the English civil war and, at 27,000 acres, constituted the second largest estate in the county. The original house was completed at the end of the seventeenth century and as the family's wealth increased, so the house was transformed into a graceful Palladian mansion. Richard Castle was responsible for the architecture in the 1730s, including the gloriously vaulted stables which are known as the equine cathedral such is their almost spiritual elegance. The contents of the house have remained intact over the years and Strokestown has thereby become a remarkable and fascinating evocation of privileged life in eighteenth century Ireland.

Inishmore *Aran Islands*

Middle Ireland

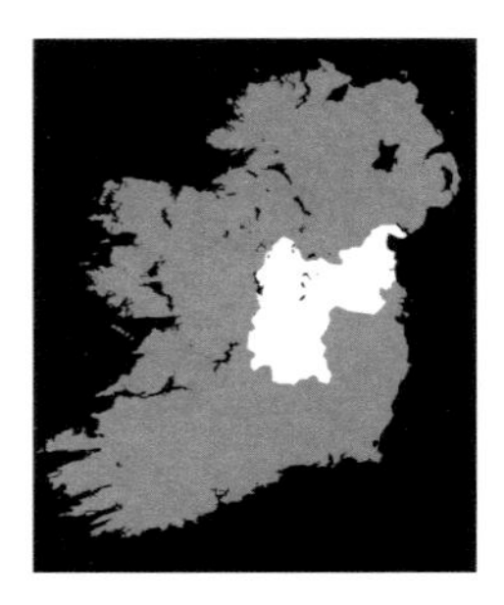

The county of Laois, (pronounced leash), lies to the south west of Dublin and should therefore have been a strong contender for membership of the Pale. As it was, Laois remained steadfastly Gaelic for much longer than other areas near the Anglo-Norman power base until the overwhelming effect of the plantations displaced the native Irish, and the county was rechristened Queen's County after Mary, the Tudor of the time and Henry VIII's daughter.

The gentle landscapes of Laois are interrupted in the west by the unspoilt and rugged Slieve Bloom Mountains, from which stupendous views sweep across all four of Ireland's modern day provinces; Ulster, Leinster, Munster and Connacht. In the north east of the county the once prosperous town of Mountmellick is a lasting memorial to an ironic anomaly in Ireland's religious conundrum; the town was founded by the unostentatious Quakers in the seventeenth century who, with many French Huguenots, escaped religious persecution in their home countries to find 'freedom of worship' in Ireland. Given the ruthless persecution of the Catholics at the time, it was hardly a phrase familiar on the streets of Ireland.

To even the marital score and match Laois's Queen's County, neighbouring Offaly was renamed King's County after Mary's husband, and is characterised by the flat plains and dank expanses of bogland that typify much of middle Ireland. Of the two great bogs in Offaly, Boora Bog to the west is the less relentlessly desolate and in fact proved the source of much anthropological excitement when it yielded evidence that even in the inhospitable environs of central Ireland, some human life had existed more than 9000 years ago. Early travel across the bogs was only practicable by means of ancient highways based on raised glacial ridges called eskers (one of the few Irish words in the English language), many of which became main routes across what was otherwise almost impenetrable terrain. Esker Riada was the Kings Road between Leinster and Connacht, and it was on this ridge that Clonmacnois, Ireland's greatest monastic site, was built in the sixth century.

Clonmacnois was founded in 545 AD by Saint Ciaran and became one of Ireland's most celebrated centres of learning and worship; when Ireland acquired the accolade throughout Europe as the Land of Saints and Scholars it was based to a large extent on the great traditions of Clonmacnois, which remained at the height of its influence until the twelfth century. Feted throughout Ireland and the western world, it was only logical that the Kings of Tara and Connacht would elect to be buried in such illustrious surroundings, and the ranks of the royal who lie within the cathedral include Rory O'Connor, the last High King of Tara, who died in 1198.

Clonmacnois

Birr Castle

Despite its isolated position on a great esker overlooking the Shannon plain, Clonmacnois was a famous prize and repeatedly devastated by first the Vikings, and then virtually every new arrival in the area until in 1552 it finally succumbed to the brutality of the Tudor regime. Despite these setbacks, until a fire wrought irreparable damage at the end of the twelfth century, the monastery and its buildings included 106 houses and 13 churches, of which the cathedral was the largest and home to the well known Whispering Door, where lepers could confess to a priest a safe distance away, their words carried by the strange acoustics of the arch.

South of Clonmacnois, the formal and fading Georgian elegance of Birr is a legacy of the Parsons family, later Earls of Rosse, who were granted the O'Carroll estate in 1620 and who planned the town to complement the magnificence of Birr Castle. The Parsons were an extraordinarily inventive and imaginative family; the second Earl of Rosse planted box hedges in his extensive gardens at the end of the eighteenth century which are now, at twelve metres, the tallest recorded anywhere; the third Earl built the largest telescope in the world in 1845, a title it retained for 75 years, another invented the steam turbine and yet another pioneered early nineteenth century photographic techniques.

Bordering onto the north of Offaly, the county of Westmeath is known for the serene nature of its loughs and productive pastureland, and also for the somewhat less than serene nature of its past history, which entailed being divided from Meath in 1542 to be administered separately, so unruly and uncontrollable were the local Gaelic chieftains.

Westmeath's loughs are famed for their fishing, and in particular for the largest trout ever caught in Ireland which was landed at Lough Ennell in 1894 and weighed an impressive 11.7 kilogrammes. More romantically, one of Ireland's most famous and tragic legends is set in the lovely surroundings of Lough Derravagh in northern Westmeath. The children of Lir were turned into golden voiced swans by their stepmother who, jealous of their father's love for them, condemned the children to spend 300 years on Lough Derravagh, 300 on the Sea of Moyle between Scotland and Ireland and another 300 on Inis Gloire. Lir was heartbroken and turned his wife into a hideous vulture, but nothing could break the spell and the children eventually died on Inis Gloire, after turning back into aged humans for the last miserable moments of their long and blighted lives.

South west of Lough Derravagh, the very centre of Ireland lies beneath the Hill of Uisneach, where the feline shaped Catstone reputedly marks the spot at which the five ancient provinces of Ireland converged. The hilltop was probably a ceremonial site where the pagan festival of Bealtaine was celebrated by the Celts every year in early May, hence becoming the Gaelic word for that month. Bealtaine was an admirable arrangement in which the commercial and the spiritual merged in a practical melange of religious ceremony and international trade fair; Mediterranean merchants exchanged exotic wares for the produce of Ireland and by all accounts a good time was had by all into the bargain.

Close by, the lively county town of Mullingar featured in several of James Joyce's novels, including A Portrait of the Artist as a Young Man and Ulysses. It was in Ulysses that the tale of a local aristocrat appears; based entirely on the truth, it involved the first Earl of Belvedere, who locked his wife in Belvedere House for unproven and probably non-existent adultery with his brother Arthur for thirty one interminable years. The same neurotic Earl fell out with another brother in the mid eighteenth century to such a degree that he went to great expense and trouble to construct a 'ruined' wall - known as the Jealous Wall - to spoil the view from his brother's estate. Eccentricity was not, however, confined merely to Belvedere; just outside Mullingar in a small Protestant churchyard, a bizarre beehive shaped tomb testifies to Adolphus Cooke's firmly held conviction that in his next reincarnation he would return as a bee; that he also believed his grandfather watched over him in the form of a turkey was perhaps an indication of his refreshingly original approach to life in general.

North of Westmeath, the watery landscapes of County Longford are endowed with wonderful fishing and are also where the shortlived Royal Canal meets the great River Shannon. The canal was built in the eighteenth century to link Dublin with the river, but by the middle of the following century had already been superseded as a means of transport by the railway boom. Oliver Goldsmith, the unconventional playwright and poet, was born in southern Longford at Pallas in 1729 and rose to great acclaim in Ireland and Britain with plays such as 'She Stoops to Conquer' and his famously poignant poem, 'Deserted Village'.

Of all the counties in Ireland, Meath probably epitomizes the idyll of rural Ireland more than any other. The quality of the soil remains undiminished and the natural riches which attracted the earliest settlers still render Meath one of Ireland's most important agricultural areas. The impossibly lush valley of the languorous River Boyne is redolent with the atmosphere of past civilisations and scattered with great houses and prehistoric ruins, of which the Bru na Boinne complex is quite unsurpassed in the world.

Amongst the many prehistoric monuments which make up this remarkable collection of tombs and stone circles, the Newgrange passage grave is Ireland's most awe-inspiring Stone Age relic. Constructed more than 5000 years ago, Newgrange predates the pyramids by several centuries, although there are basic similarities in that both were built to honour the dead by relatively sophisticated peoples nurtured on fertile river flood plains. Under the vast 80 metre diameter mound covering the tomb, a long passage leads to a tall vaulted central chamber, which is decorated with the flamboyant whirling spirals often to be found in passage grave culture and which have exercised the minds of generations of observers as to their significance.

But Newgrange was not just an impressive physical statement; it was a site of the utmost sanctity in pagan times and one in which the winter solstice played a pivotal role. On December 21, just as the sun rises, a beam of light enters the grave through a precisely aligned slit in the roof and edges slowly down the passage, finally reaching the central chamber where it bursts into a flare of light, illuminating the darkness for a few short minutes until the beam recedes, leaving the tomb black and silent. Dramatic and eerie though the entire process is, it is slightly later than the actual moment of sunrise; rather than an inexactitude in Neolithic calculation, it transpires that the earth's position has shifted slightly since Newgrange was built and the solstice observed.

Near Newgrange, the Battle of the Boyne was fought and won by the Protestant William of Orange in 1690, whose symbolic victory over the Catholics signified a radical change in the religious stakes in Ireland. Twelve centuries earlier, Saint Patrick chose the Hill of Slane to throw down a symbolic gauntlet to the pagan Celts by lighting a Pascal fire on Easter Day within sight of the Royal Hill of Tara. Given the coincidence of Easter with a prominent pagan festival, and no doubt fully aware of the fact that it was strictly forbidden to light a fire before that on Tara, Saint Patrick had yet again shown his predilection for dramatic gesture. He was invited to explain himself to the High King, at which meeting the earthquake he summoned to subdue the guards may have been a persuading factor, but the upshot was that he was allowed to preach the Christian word to the King's cohorts; in memory of this momentous occasion, a fire is still lit on the hill by a priest on the eve of every Easter Sunday.

Slieve Bloom mountains

For many centuries, the Hill of Tara was the seat of the High Kings of Ireland, whose position, whilst certainly not omnipotent, was as close to supreme power as existed in a country of petty Kingdoms. Although physical evidence of Tara's sanctity and political importance is almost entirely lacking, there is undoubtedly a potent aura that pervades the lovely hill and its surroundings; the ancient legends that mention Tara are legion and the stories of Druids, pagan worship and goddess Queens rest as easily on the landscapes of Tara as the tales of Christian High Kings and their followers.

North west of Tara on the River Blackwater, the monastery of Kells was established by Saint Columba in the sixth century. It was here that the exquisite masterpiece of Celtic Art, the Book of Kells, was brought for safekeeping from the Viking plagued monastery on Iona in Scotland. As a sanctuary Kells, or Ceanannus Mor, was not an entirely successful choice, for the Vikings sacked the monastery on at least five occasions before the Normans arrived and continued the tradition. Nonetheless, the Book of Kells miraculously survived to become one of the wonders of Christianity, despite a hiccup in which it was stolen and later found abandoned in a bog. The thief had apparently only been interested in the gold case in which the book was kept.

Louth, which lies on the coast between Meath and Northern Ireland, is the smallest county in the land. Size notwithstanding, it was the setting of one of the oldest stories in any

European language, the Cattle Raid of Cooley, and the stage on which some of Ireland's bloodiest history was played out. The town of Drogheda gained its name from the bridge which connected the two Viking settlements on either side of the river; Droichead Atha meaning bridge of the ford. By the fourteenth century it was not only one of the most important towns in Ireland, but also a frontier town on the Pale. In 1649 Cromwell perpetrated his most notorious massacre there, killing 3000 native Irish and Old English Catholics at the start of his campaign to crush Ireland into submission.

Just to the north, the ruins of the glorious Mellifont Abbey are all that remain of Ireland's first Cistercian monastery. In the early days of the twelfth century, Saint Malachy, despairing of the profligacy and moral laxness of the Gaelic monasteries, travelled to France and seeing the purity of the Cistercian monks at Clairvaux, determined to found a monastery of the order in Ireland. In 1142, Mellifont came into being, sounding the death knell of the rather jolly Irish system and instigating an austerity and harshness which never found a spiritual home in the Irish culture. It also signified a new approach to monastic architecture; the haphazard arrangements of Irish monasteries being replaced by formal and strictly organised layouts.

Close by, the ruins of Monasterboice exude a compelling stillness, an atmosphere that is heightened by the stark outlines of some of Ireland's finest High Crosses. Monasterboice was founded around the fourth century by Saint Buithe, who reputedly gave his name to the River Boyne, although it no doubt predated Christianity as a pagan site in earlier times. High Crosses, like round towers, are so typical of Irish Christian architecture as to be almost national symbols and the art of the High Cross reached its zenith in the tenth century, teaching the illiterate public biblical stories in a form that was easily understood and, significantly, largely resistant to Viking removal or destruction. The stone carvings and intricate Celtic designs found on Muiredach's Cross at Monasterboice render it one of the finest examples of Celtic art, whilst the ornate West Cross, standing 6.5 metres high, is one of the tallest High Crosses in Ireland.

In the north of Louth, Ardee and the lonely emptiness of the Cooley Peninsula are the territory of the great Irish legend, the Cattle Raid of Cooley, in which Queen Maeve of Connacht sets her heart on snatching the famous brown bull of Ulster to equal her husband's fine white animal. Druid spells and trickery abound, and although her army is single handedly defeated by the Hound of Ulster, Cuchulainn, his compatriots having been smitten with a mysterious illness, Maeve finally finds her prize and takes it back to compare with the beautiful white bull, whereupon the brown slays the white and dies of exhaustion from galloping all over Ireland. And no doubt therein lies a moral.

Counties Monaghan and Cavan share a common history in that they were part of the province of Ulster before partition left them in the Republic of Ireland. Whilst Monaghan is scattered with rounded drumlins, the scenery of Cavan is pockmarked with a multitude of loughs.

Monagham was relatively untouched by the plantations until Cromwell distributed the local lands to Puritans and Scottish Presbyterians in the mid seventeenth century. Their simple and grave approach to life is still apparent in many of the towns, as is an element of Scottish dourness, but nonetheless Monaghan thrived in the eighteenth and nineteenth centuries from the lace and linen making industries. In Carrickmacross, a castle built in the 1630s by the third Earl of Essex, the nuns of St Louise Convent have revived the skills of making hand made lace, some of which adorned the wedding dress of the late Diana, Princess of Wales.

Muiredach's Cross *Monasterboice*

Sligo, Leitrim, and Donegal

Sligo is a county of unexpected charm and beauty, where the fishing is wonderful, the coast and beaches magnificent and the concentration of remarkable antiquities greater than anywhere else in Ireland. Much of the scenery consists of gentle rolling landscapes, across which great vistas stretch towards distant mountains and silent loughs bathed in the wonderful light that is so typical of the west coast of Ireland.

However, Sligo is not only captivating physically: it also has the most romantic of literary and artistic connections. The Yeats brothers, who spent much of their childhood there, were bewitched by the county and its legends to the extent that Jack, the artist, declared that he 'never did a painting without putting a thought of Sligo into it'.

William Butler Yeats, his more famous brother, was born in Dublin, but it was undoubtedly Sligo that had the most profound influence upon him. His poems and writing frequently alluded to the county and he is commemorated in the town of Sligo by a statue inscribed with the chilling and memorable lines he wrote to describe the reversal in public attitude towards Republicanism after the 1916 Easter Rising. 'All changed, changed utterly; A terrible beauty is born.' Yeats was a leading light in the Gaelic literary revival, an ardent supporter of the cause for Irish independence and in 1923 he received the Nobel Prize for literature. Although he died in France, he was finally buried in the shadow of his beloved Ben Bulben mountain with the simple epitaph he wrote for himself, 'Cast a cold eye on life, on death, Horsemen, pass by.'

The town of Sligo has been pre-eminent in the north west since the partition of Ireland left Derry, or Londonderry depending on your political standpoint, as part of Northern Ireland. Sligo was first sacked by the Vikings at the start of the ninth century and, as was the norm in Irish history, settled by the Anglo-Normans in 1245 in the guise of Maurice Fitzgerald, Earl of Kildare. Unusually, however, the Anglo-Normans never established a firm foothold and so Sligo remained under predominantly Gaelic influence until the Tudors took control at the end of the sixteenth century. Thereafter the set pattern was re-established and Sligo suffered the usual fate of Irish towns by being devastated by Cromwell in the 1640s. Nonetheless, it was the last of the western Jacobite garrisons to fall to the Williamite forces after the Battle of the Boyne, and despite the damage inflicted over the centuries, still retains an air of prosperity and antiquity.

Sligo was never a well populated country and the plantations were not therefore as traumatic as in other parts of Ireland where displacement was more of an issue. English and Scottish

Sligo Town *the art gallery*

families slid into Sligo society reasonably peacefully and the Gaelic tradition remained a vibrant force until the Great Famine devastated the Irish population by starvation or emigration. As a result, Gaelic ceased to be the spoken language and much of the local folklore and culture would have been irrevocably lost had it not been for the work of such devotees as Yeats and Lady Gregory.

Not far from Sligo town an extraordinary collection of passage tombs, dolmens and more than sixty stone circles make up Carrowmore cemetery, one of the largest and most impressive megalithic burial sites in Europe. Nearby, the legendary Queen Maeve of Connacht was reputedly buried in the enormous cairn at the summit of Knocknarea Mountain. The mountain is a majestic landmark in itself, but the fact that the cairn was covered with what is estimated to be 40,000 tons of earth and rocks in Neolithic times must have been an undertaking that defies contemplation. That these pre-historic people who made such prolific use of large stones in their architecture for the dead left no comparable record of how they lived is a fascinating reflection on the store they set on the afterlife in comparison with the present.

Just inland from Sligo Bay, Lough Gill was one of Yeats' favourite spots; the tranquil reaches surrounded by wooded banks featured in many of his poems, perhaps the loveliest of which describes the tiny lake isle of Innisfree with some of his most seductive words. Perhaps he was referring to the inevitable legend associated with the lough which had a Dominican monk throwing a silver bell into the water, the tones of which are only audible to the pure and free from sin.

North of Lough Gill the sixth century remains of a monastery at Drumcliff bear witness to the exploits of St Columba, Prince of Tyrconnel, which prompted him to leave Ireland for voluntary exile on the Scottish island of Iona. The story goes that Columba borrowed a psalter from St Finian and made a copy of it without asking permission. Finian was outraged and took the matter to the High King who ordered that Columba return the offending article forthwith with the words, 'to every cow its calf, to every book its copy'. Columba refused, the ensuing battle resulted in more than 3000 deaths and, having built the monastery as penance, he left for Iona to convert as many souls as had been slain as a result of his obstinacy.

The Gore-Booth family, whose family home of Lissadell lies nearby, were also no strangers to obstinacy. Constance Gore-Booth, later Countess Markievicz, was reprieved from the death sentence for her involvement in the Easter Rising and subsequently refused to take up her seat in the British Parliament having been elected as an MP for Sinn Fein. Of her forebears, Constance's grandfather, Sir Robert, was also an exceptional man; he mortgaged the house during the Great Famine to provide food for the starving and the inscription 'clock paid for by the tenants of Ballymote Estate in gratitude to Sir Robert Gore-Booth' in Ballymote Church is one of the very few genuine tributes in Ireland to the landlords of that awful time.

Lying alongside Sligo, County Leitrim is, like its neighbour, renowned for excellent fishing. Dividing the county nearly in half is Lough Allen, and whilst the lush scenery of the south is dominated by the Shannon, the north is a landscape of mountains and glens. Before the Tudors renamed it, Leitrim was called Breffni and ruled by the O'Rourke family. It was Tiernan O'Rourke's wife, Devorgilla who, by eloping with Dermot MacMurrough from Dromahair Castle in the twelfth century, inadvertently altered the entire course of Irish history. His treacherous plea for help from the English to fight the furious O'Rourke led to the first Anglo-Norman invasion of Ireland; the rest is history, but it is ironic that Anglo-Norman influence was initially concentrated in the south, the north remaining predominantly Gaelic until the turmoil of the sixteenth century.

'I will arise and go now,
and go to Innisfree ...
And I shall have some peace there,
for peace comes dropping slow,
Dropping from the veils of the morning
to where the cricket sings.'

One of the greatest Gaelic traditions was that of court musicians sustained by the patronage of the Gaelic chieftains. After their exodus in the Flight of the Earls, patronage went into gradual decline until Turlough O'Carolan, the blind Leitrim born composer and harpist, became the last of the court bards to eke a living from the dying Gaelic system. The Rebellion of 1798, the Penal Laws and eventually famine devastated Gaelic music in Ireland, which was, nonetheless, carried abroad with the emigrants of the 'Irish diaspora' to return, embellished, to what is now a thriving traditional music scene.

Bundoran

On the Leitrim shore of Lough Gill, Parke's Castle is built on the foundations of the stronghold of Brian O'Rourke, last native chieftain of Breffni. In 1588, O'Rourke was one of the few who offered help and shelter to Spaniards shipwrecked in the Armada, for which gesture he was executed for high treason at Tyburn; as a Spanish officer observed, 'Although this chief is a savage, he is a good Christian and an enemy of the heretics and is always at war with them'. The new castle was built by Parke in the 1620s in typical planter style; defence was, as observed by the Spaniard, a priority and the restored castle retains a steadfastly invincible appearance.

Bundoran lies on the tiny stretch of land that connects the county of Donegal to the Republic of Ireland. The county's geographical position relative to Northern Ireland is by all accounts bizarre, and arose in the partition of Ireland when Edward Carson, leader of the Unionists, left Donegal in the south believing that had it been included in the north, the Catholic majority would soon have voted Northern Ireland out of existence.

County Donegal was originally called Tyrconnel until the name was changed by the British to that of their garrison. It is one of the most magnificent and varied counties in Ireland, in which the landscapes vary from the highest and most dramatic cliffs in Europe to soft purple heather moors and brown bogs, from the oldest mountains in Ireland to the rich pastures of the east: it is said that some of the most beautiful scenery in Ireland is to be found in Donegal.

Donegal town was settled by the Vikings in the early ninth century, hence it acquired the name which means 'fort of the stranger'. Once Gaelic society had reasserted itself, the O'Donnells controlled the town and area until the seventeenth century, fighting interminably with the O'Neills of Ulster until they joined forces in common opposition to the English. As was often the case in the plantation era, the 'Diamond' or town square was built in the shadow of the castle to enable the British to keep control over any rowdiness that arose from the fairs and events taking place. In Donegal's Diamond, an obelisk commemorates the prescient and scholarly Franciscan friars who, anticipating the imminent demise of Gaelic culture, wrote 'The Annals of the Four Masters' in 1623. Documenting what was known of Celtic legend, mythology and culture, the Annals are a priceless record of Irish history, the first entry being a note of Noah's granddaughter's visit to Ireland in 2958 BC, the last dated 1618.

In complete contrast to the gentle beauty and tranquillity of Lough Derg to the east of Donegal town, the spectacular grandeur of the cliffs of Slieve League on the Atlantic Coast is both blatant and awe inspiring. From the top of what are the highest marine cliffs in Europe the sound of crashing breakers hundreds of metres below is eerily muffled and it is apparently possible on a clear day to see almost a third of Ireland. Despite the fact that Slieve League means grey mountain, the colour of the rock face changes from white to amber to red in the precipitous fall to the sea creating an effect which at sunset is absolutely breathtaking.

At Slieve League

Silver Strand *Malinbeg*

In the north of Donegal, the Derryveagh mountains yield spectacular views to the coast and inland whilst Mount Errigal is reputedly one of the loveliest mountains in Ireland; cone shaped and often swathed in mist, it has an almost mythical beauty which seems entirely appropriate in such enchanting landscapes. Close by, Lough Gartan and its shores are also extraordinarily beautiful, as befits the birthplace of one of Ireland's most revered saints. Columba was born of royal blood in Gartan in 521 AD and the Natal stone on which he first opened his eyes is still venerated by expectant mothers praying for a safe delivery. The Flagstone of Loneliness on which he slept is supposed to cure sorrows, and during Ireland's long history of emigration many a sad prospective traveller has laid his head on the flagstone before leaving in the hope of alleviating the pangs of homesickness.

The north coast of Donegal is a convoluted and dramatic series of headlands, sea loughs and sweeping golden beaches. At the southern end of Sheep Haven Bay lie the romantic ruins of Doe Castle, fifteenth century stronghold of the McSwineys who were part of a Scottish contingent imported by the Gaelic chieftains to defend Ireland against the Anglo-Normans. Known as gallowglasses, these mercenary soldiers were instrumental in preserving the Gaelic kingdoms until the forces of Elizabeth I proved overwhelming at the end of the sixteenth century, and given this connection it is perhaps not surprising that at times the local Gaelic dialect seems to have more in common with Scottish Gaelic than with that of the south.

The culmination of Elizabeth's campaign to bring Ireland under English control was the Flight of the Earls in 1607; 'Now stolen is the soul from Eire's breast' was no understatement of the impact on traditional Gaelic society, and it was from Rathmullen on Lough Swilly that Rory O'Donnel, Earl of Tyrconnel and Hugh O'Neill, Earl of Tyrone left the country forever after signing the death warrant of Gaelic Ireland with the Treaty of Mellifont.

On the opposite side of Lough Swilly, the rugged Inishowen Peninsula reaches to Ireland's most northerly point at the towering bluff of Malin Head. Once a separate kingdom and controlled by the O'Doherty clan, Inishowen has an uplifting scenic beauty which is crowned by the glorious Grianan of Aileach fort. Dating originally from 1700 BC, the 'sun palace on Aileach' was the seat of the O'Neills for centuries and the setting for Saint Patrick's baptism of Eoghan, founder of the clan, in the fifth century. Emanating from the fort is an intriguing sense of power and antiquity that is heightened by the stupendous views in all directions and the unproven theory that there are secret underground passages running from beneath the Hill of Aileach to Scalp Mountain six miles away.

Northern Ireland

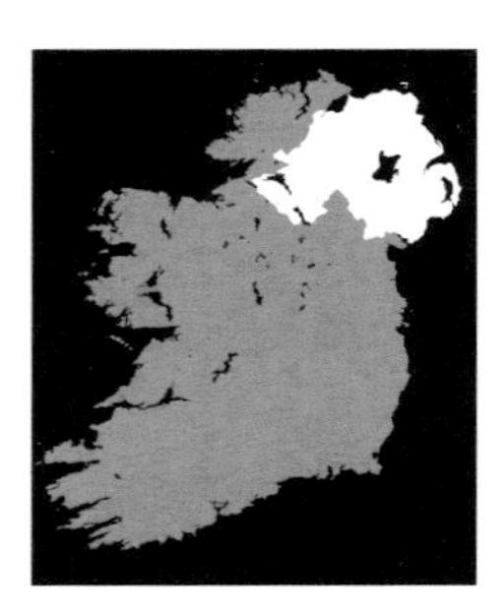

Northern Ireland, which comprises six of the nine original counties of Ulster, came into being after the 1921 Anglo-Irish Treaty led to the division of Ireland into Protestant dominated Northern Ireland and the predominantly Catholic Republic of Ireland. The north remains part of the United Kingdom with a bond the Unionist Protestants are determined to maintain, but which diametrically opposes the ambitions of the Nationalists and Republican Catholics who fervently wish for an independent and united Ireland.

The resulting 'troubles' in the province have frequently overshadowed the great and varied beauty of the Ulster landscapes, which sweep from bucolic farmlands to the fantastical geometry of Giant's Causeway, from the compelling desolation of the Sperrin mountains to the idyllic splendour of Lough Erne. Overlaid on the country, the imprint of Ulster's history is clearly cast in the prehistoric sites, ruined castles and plantation towns which abound throughout the region. The mysterious Celtic civilisation, the Viking and Anglo-Norman invasions, the plantations and the linen trade, which figured so greatly in the economy of eighteenth century Ulster, have all left a legacy which is not only visually spectacular, but which does much to explain Ireland's turbulent past.

The capital of Northern Ireland is Belfast, which originated as a tiny settlement by the now subterranean River Farset, whence came the name Beal Feirste, meaning 'mouth of the sandy ford'. Until the end of the seventeenth century Belfast remained little more than a riverside hamlet despite several false starts, the first of which was the arrival of the omnipresent Anglo-Norman Baron, John de Courcy, who built a castle by the River Lagan in 1177 in a shortlived attempt to establish a local power base that lasted less than twenty years. Thereafter the mighty O'Neill clan controlled the area until the English gained the upper hand over Red Hugh O'Neill in 1603 and forced him to relinquish authority over Ulster.

Almost immediately, Sir Arthur Chichester was sent at James I's behest to 'plant' Belfast which, in spite of being granted a charter by the king, still remained a backwater until, at the end of the seventeenth century an influx of French Protestant Huguenots fleeing religious persecution in France brought with them the sophisticated linen weaving skills which were to prove so vital to Belfast's future. They were soon followed by thousands of English and Scottish Presbyterian planters, whose influence ultimately created a city which at times seemed more British than Irish and which provoked such acidic judgements as, 'the town and its neighbouring districts have nothing in common with the rest of Ireland.'

Antrim *Glenarriff*

Ironically, during the eighteenth century Belfast was well known for the unusual degree of mutual religious tolerance that existed in the city, to the extent that in 1791 it was the birthplace of the Society of United Irishmen, founded by a group of Belfast Presbyterians to unite both creeds in a common Irish nationality. Despite the best intentions, the movement culminated in disaster and Belfast lurched into sectarianism with a divide that was exacerbated during the nineteenth century and which has since widened into the bitter antagonism of today.

Meanwhile the industrial revolution, which had little impact elsewhere in Ireland, was creating a golden era in Belfast. The ship building, ropemaking and linen industries flourished, fuelling the phenomenal transformation of Belfast from a small town in 1800 into 'Linenopolis', a grandiose and confident Victorian metropolis. In 1888 Queen Victoria granted the town city status, eliciting a gratitude from the city fathers that was manifested in a plethora of monuments and streets built or named in her honour, and in the latter half of the nineteenth century Belfast went from strength to strength, outstripping many of its British rivals and maintaining impetus into the twentieth century long after many other industrial cities had lost momentum.

Of the great legacies of Belfast's glorious Victorian era, the Harland and Wolff shipyards, which were established in 1859 and built the ill-fated Titanic, numbered amongst the leading shipyards of the world in their heyday and still dominate the skyline of modern Belfast with two of the largest cranes ever built. At the opposite, more relaxed extreme of Victorian splendour the ever popular and unashamedly over the top Crown Liquor Saloon remains a flamboyantly atmospheric and opulent gin palace in which the magnificent Victorian decor stands unaltered and which epitomises Belfast's welcoming and hospitable spirit.

Spirit and humour are great Irish attributes which are well illustrated in the fate of the Giant's Ring, an enormous megalithic site just south of Belfast. Two hundred metres in diameter and surrounded by a high earthen rim, its physical attributes were not lost on the eighteenth century folk of Belfast, who, in a wonderful display of irreverence, used what was no doubt a site of immense importance as a race track.

Reaching away from Belfast, the Ards Peninsula curves southwards to enclose the great expanse of Strangford Lough, so called by the Vikings whose regard for the racing current which pulls the tide through the narrows at the seaward end led them to conclude that the name 'strong fjord' was more than apposite. The peninsula and the coast below it are scattered with a myriad of castle ruins, many of them the tower houses so typical of Irish strongholds in mediaeval times. Kilclief is but one of a great chain of castles guarding the strait below Strangford and is the oldest tower house in the county, built by the adulterous, and later defrocked, Bishop of Down in the early half of the fifteenth century.

The Crown Liquor Saloon

Belfast

To the south, the country's early history becomes inextricably linked with St Patrick; his first Irish landfall as a missionary was in Strangford Lough in 432AD and unintentional though it may have been, to the people of County Down it was a great boon. His first convert in Ireland was the local chieftain at Saul, whose new found Christian status induced him to part with one of his sheep shelters as a makeshift base for the Saint. This was more than slightly ironic in that St Patrick had once been abducted by the Irish and put to work as a slave tending sheep; however, the shelter became St Patrick's first church, the village claimed its name from the Gaelic word for barn, Sabhal, and it was here, reputedly, that he died in 491AD, having made remarkable inroads into the conversion of not only Ulster, but the whole of Ireland. Legend has it that St Patrick was finally buried in Downpatrick, a claim hotly contested by Armagh, after a host of angels led an ox cart carrying his body to the cathedral on the Hill of Down. The hill was an ancient site of immense strategic importance and the cathedral, which was itself frequently attacked and reconstructed like most religious foundations, was built within the ruins of an impressive fort, whence arose the name Dun (fort) Padriag, or Downpatrick, and, coincidentally, the name County Down.

To the west of the pretty village of Strangford which stands sentinel over the entrance to Strangford Lough lies the vast estate of Castle Ward, Ireland's equivalent of Glyndebourne. Every June, opera lovers can ponder the strange marriage of Lord and Lady Bangor, whose deep seated incompatibility in all respects led not only to their ultimate divorce, but also the creation of a wonderfully schizophrenic house in 1760. His love of classical Palladian won the day for the facade and her taste for the neo-Gothic found expression at the rear, whilst within the house the dichotomy of their taste is still reflected in the bizarre juxtaposition of decoration and furnishings which veer from the stately to the whimsical.

To the west of Down, beyond the Gap of the North which lies between the windswept emptiness of the Mourne Mountains and the magical beauty of Slieve Gullion, Armagh is a county of great loveliness, especially in the spring when it earns its sobriquet of the 'garden of Ulster' from the swathes of apple blossom which adorn the many orchards. The elegant Georgian town of Armagh was probably the earliest settlement in Ireland and named after the magnificent Queen Macha, whose base on the hill in the first millennium BC became known as Ard Macha or Macha's height. In the fifth century St Patrick established the first Christian bishopric in Armagh and, having again successfully converted a local landowning chieftain, acquired the hilltop on which he subsequently founded a cathedral. For the fifteen intervening centuries since then, a cathedral has stood on the hill and it is a matter of some pride to the Irish that it therefore predates Canterbury Cathedral. The fact that Armagh is the seat of both the Archbishop of the Church of Ireland and the Catholic primacy of all Ireland, coupled with the convenient geological fact of being surrounded, with a stretch of the imagination, by seven small hills, has led the town to declare itself, perhaps a little optimistically, as the Rome of Ireland.

By the eighth century, Armagh had become a beacon in the Land of Saints and Scholars and was renowned throughout Europe for its religious and cultural standing. Such a reputation, however, soon proved a double edged sword by attracting the unwelcome attention of Viking raiders who raided and plundered the town with monotonous regularity. Armagh survived these and frequent subsequent attacks until the sixteenth century Reformation, during which much of the town was destroyed as the Irish and the English fought for supremacy. It was the final straw and so it was that the English and Scottish settlers who arrived in the seventeenth century plantations therefore had more or less a blank canvas on which to work. By the latter half of the eighteenth century Armagh had been reinvented into an gracious Georgian town with a flourishing linen industry. Richard Robinson, Francis Johnston, one of Ireland's pre-eminent architects and himself an Armagh man, and Richard Castle were largely responsible for the dignified and well proportioned architecture, much of which was constructed from the warmly hued sandstone known as 'Armagh marble'.

Just west of Armagh lies the Navan Fort, a powerfully atmospheric Iron and Bronze Age site

Navan Fort

which became the ancient and mystical capital of the north and a seat of supreme power which rivalled that of Tara. Shown on Ptolemy's map of 140 AD as Isamnion, the Navan Fort was Ireland's Camelot, for centuries the seat of the Kings of Ulster and their court of the Knights of the Red Branch. Of these illustrious warriors Cuchulainn was the greatest; a valiant hero and champion whose noble deeds were forever preserved in Irish mythology in the Ulster Cycle of legendary tales.

It was to the north of the Protestant enclave of nearby Loughall that in 1795 a clash between the Protestant Peep'O'Day Boys and the Catholic Defenders prompted the formation of what is now the Orange Order. Victorious after what became known as the 'Battle of the Diamond', the Peep'O'Day Boys formed the society to defend Protestantism, even though the battle was more of a local skirmish than a political or ideological confrontation. Named after William of Orange, the Orange Order became a considerable force in Northern Ireland in the nineteenth century and as a secret political society with Masonic overtones was, and still is, viewed with some caution by those outside its Lodges.

County Fermanagh is the smallest of Northern Ireland's counties and belies even that size with the fact that a third of its area consists of loughs and rivers. Fermanagh's greatest glory

Enniskillen

The Watergate

is the magnificent Lough Erne, an 80 kilometre stretch of water surrounded by spectacular landscapes, on which the reflections of the sky mirrored on a calm day make for a scene that is utterly spellbinding. Lower Lough Erne is a magical sight, dotted with wooded islands on which intriguing Celtic and early Christian ruins hint at the past importance of the Lough as a principle highway from the coast into the heart of Ireland.

Fermanagh's history was, not surprisingly, greatly influenced by the Lough and its surrounding complex of waterways. It was difficult terrain for invaders to penetrate especially given that many Celts and early Christians lived on isolated and easily defended crannogs, or artificial islands, built on tree trunks driven into the bottom of the lough and connected to dry land by a twisting underwater causeway, if at all. External influence therefore filtered only slowly through to Fermanagh and although Christianity did gradually enter the local culture, many relics of the time point to a lengthy period in which paganism and Christianity were fused.

Fermanagh subsequently proved remarkably resistant to invasion by the Vikings, the Anglo-Normans, and, until the end of the fifteenth century, the English. But the English were hellbent on controlling the whole of Ireland and Enniskillen, situated on an island in the narrow waist separating Upper and Lower Lough Erne, was a vital strategic point, guarding as it did one of only three access routes from the south into Ulster - the others being on the west coast at the mouth of the River Erne or through the Gap of the North in the east. Although the town was valiantly defended by the Irish, the English campaign finally paid dividends and in 1600 Enniskillen fell. The planters arrived soon afterwards, but nonetheless the English were compelled to build a ring of castles around the Lough to maintain some semblance of control over the unruly locals.

North of Fermanagh, County Tyrone was the base of the O'Neills of Ulster, all-powerful Earls of Tyrone until the Treaty of Mellifont abolished their authority, and Red Hugh, the last King of Ulster who fled the country in the Flight of the Earls in 1607. It was the O'Neill clan which first adopted the Red Hand of Ulster, symbol of Northern Ireland, as their emblem; no doubt they approved of its gory provenance which involved a race for Ireland won by the Viking chief who cut off his own hand and threw it ashore to reach land before his rival claimant.

Tyrone was once a prominent centre of the linen industry, which formed one of the mainstays of the Ulster economy in the eighteenth and nineteenth centuries. Scant evidence now remains of what was once a thriving industry, although Wellbrook Beetling Mill and Sion Mills linen village are fascinating reminders of a way of life that has long since vanished. Linen is produced from flax, which flourished in the Irish climate and, once harvested, was dried in the open before the seed was removed to make linseed oil. Bundles of flax were then soaked for up to two weeks to soften the outer stem and 'scutched' to separate the stem from the fibres, which were finally spun and woven into lengths of cloth. Unbleached linen was sold through brown linen halls, whilst bleached linen, which was soaked and laid out in great lengths to whiten in the sun on bleaching greens, was smoothed by hammering with 'beetle' hammers, and sold through white linen halls, many of which are still to be seen throughout the country.

In the north east of Tyrone lie the lonely gold bearing Sperrin Mountains, the lower reaches of which are partly covered in woodland whilst the upper reaches are clad in heather or blanket bog. These blanket bogs cover hills and valleys and grow only in climates wet enough to guarantee more than a depressing 240 days of rain a year. Almost a fifth of Ireland was once covered by bogs which evolved over tens of thousands of years but which were traditionally seen as either an inconvenience or, at best, a source of peat fuel. That bogs are now a focus for conservationists is often a subject of wry humour in Ireland given their possibly apocryphal role in portraying a less than glamourous image for the Irish.

Reaching up to the north coast, County Derry was the region of Ulster most extensively settled by English and Scottish planters in the early years of the seventeenth century and was originally planted under the auspices of the wealthy Merchant Guilds of London. As a result the county is scattered with plantation towns built by the guilds and occasionally, as in the case of Draperstown, named after them.

In the sixth century St Columba founded a monastery in the town of Derry which was named 'Daire Colmcille', meaning oak grove of Columba, and which was subsequently shortened and anglicised to Derry. Despite a deeply entrenched resistance to English domination, Derry was finally planted in 1609 and soon became known as Londonderry due to the involvement of the London guilds. The town layout and magnificent city walls, which were

Giant's Causeway

built between 1613 and 1618, have survived intact and Derry's nickname of the Maiden City arose in direct reference to the fact that the walls were never breached, even in 1688 when Derry was besieged by the Catholic forces of James II after the famous apprentice boys slammed the city gates shut in his face. However, a cannon shell which was catapulted into the city offering terms of surrender to the beleaguered Protestants now resides in the porch of St Columb's Cathedral, the memorable response to which, and similar offers, being that the feisty Protestants would rather eat the Catholics and then each other than surrender.

In the nineteenth century Derry became one of the main ports for the massive exodus of the Irish to America and a successful transatlantic trade in shirts and collars developed in tandem after Will Scott invented the first industrial system of shirt manufacture. In a fine display of commercial nous Derry apparently provided shirts and uniforms for both sides in the American Civil War and in a quirky gesture which harks back to that era, still presents the American President twelve free shirts a year as a gift.

Of the six counties of Ulster, Antrim undoubtedly has the most dramatic and spectacular scenery. The Glens of Antrim on the north east coast are quite breathtakingly beautiful, but it is the Giant's Causeway, one of the great wonders of the natural world and an extraordinary phenomenon of physical chemistry, that is Antrim's most outstanding feature. The Causeway consists of nearly forty thousand polygonal columns which are almost surreal in the perfection of their geometry and were formed as laval basalt crystallised after an underground fissure erupted 60 million years ago. Less prosaically, legend has it that the giant Finn MacCool built the causeway between Ireland and the Scottish island of Staffa, where similar columns line the shore, to reach the giantess who lived there and with whom he was deeply in love.

Just south of the coast on the River Bush, Bushmills distillery is the oldest legal distillery in the world which still produces whiskey. It is a moot point whether the process of whiskey distillation was invented in Scotland or Ireland, but by the thirteenth century Irish monks were certainly adept at producing 'uisgebeatha', the water of life. Irish whiskey, with an 'e', is different not only in spelling from its Scottish counterpart, but also in the fact that it is distilled three times rather than twice to produce the velvety smoothness so characteristic of what Bushmills has been making legally since 1608, and in all probability illegally for many years before that.

On the border of Antrim, Lough Neagh is the largest lake in Ireland and Britain and is a fisherman's dream; the waters teem with trout, salmon, and 'dollaghan', a salmon like fish which grows by a covetable 3 pounds a year. It is a matter of Irish record that the lough was formed when the giant of causeway fame, Finn MacCool, hurled a handful of earth from the landscape and threw it into the sea in a raging fury. The Isle of Man was the result in the Irish sea - its similarity of shape and size are indisputable - whilst the lough was his gift to Ulster.

Picture credits

p1 Kee Wi Photo p5 Kee Wi Photo p6 Kee Wi Photo p8 Mark Fiennes
p9 Bridgeman/Private collection p10 Bridgeman/Lambeth Palace Library
p11 Bridgeman/Agnew & Sons p12 Bridgeman/Fine-Lines Fine Art
p13 Bridgeman/Private collection p14 Bridgeman/The Stapleton Collection p15 Mark Fiennes
p17 Bridgeman/Victoria Art Gallery, Bath p18 Mark Fiennes p19 Mark Fiennes
p20 Mark Fiennes p22 Bridgeman/Victoria & Albert Museum p24 Mark Fiennes
p27 Northern Irish Tourist Board p29 Kee Wi Photo p33 Mark Fiennes
p34 Bridgeman/Phillips Int'l Fine Art Auctioneers p36 Mark Fiennes p37 Mark Fiennes
p38 Mark Fiennes p41 Kee Wi Photo p42 Kee Wi Photo p45 Bridgeman/Christie's London
p47 Kee Wi Photo p49 Kee Wi Photo p50 Kee Wi Photo p53 Kee Wi Photo
p55 Kee Wi Photo p57 Kee Wi Photo p58 Kee Wi Photo p59 Kee Wi Photo
p61 Kee Wi Photo p62 Bord Fáilte Photo pp64/65 Bord Fáilte Photo p66 Bord Fáilte Photo
p67 Bridgeman/Private collection p69 Bord Fáilte Photo p71 Kee Wi Photo p72 Kee Wi Photo
p75 Kee Wi Photo p77 Bord Fáilte Photo p79 Bord Fáilte Photo p81 Bord Fáilte Photo
p82 Bord Fáilte Photo p83 Bord Fáilte Photo p84 Bord Fáilte Photo
p87 Northern Irish Tourist Board p89 Northern Irish Tourist Board
p91 Northern Irish Tourist Board p92 Northern Irish Tourist Board
p93 Northern Irish Tourist Board p95 Northern Irish Tourist Board

Ptarmigan Publishing Ltd
Growers Court
New Road
Bromham, Chippenham
Wiltshire SN15 2JA

Telephone: 01380 -859983
Facsimile: 01380 -859682

Printed by Sceptre Litho, Leicester